LIFE LESSONS
From The COCKPIT

Captivating Stories Of a BlackHawk Pilot

Tips For Your Success

FRANK VAN BUREN

FAULKS FARM PUBLISHING

Faulks Farm Publishing | Wingate North Carolina

Printed in the United States of America

Paperback ISBN: 978-1-7337269-0-0

Ebook ISBN: 978-1-7337269-1-7

TABLE OF CONTENTS

DEDICATION

This book is dedicated to my parents, George and Rena Van Buren, who raised us with the core values of patriotism and optimism. Both had served our country during World War II, at a time when they were designated as second-class citizens and didn't have the right to vote. Yet, they still believed in the future of this nation.

My father and his brother, James Van Buren, answered the call for volunteers in the early 1940s. Both were student-athletes at Howard University and stepped forward to be trained as Army Officers in the segregated units headed for the war.

My father survived the war and went on to serve the nation for 36 years. Dad participated in World War II and Korea, before the passage of the Civil Rights (1964) and Voting Rights Acts (1965). He was an extraordinary patriot, and buried with full military honors at Arlington National Cemetery in 1988.

My uncle, Second Lieutenant James Van Buren, died at a young age during the North African Campaign in World War II, and was buried in the U.S. National Cemetery in Tunisia, North Africa.

As a reflection of the slow war-mail system of the day, it took several months for the news of his death to reach my father in the European Theater of Operations. The process culminated with a gut-wrenching, but inspiring letter written in 1943 from my grandfather to my father.

The letter ends with the following passage: "And now my son you are all I have left and I pray God to send you back. Keep your chin up because this is war and we must expect anything to happen. May God comfort you. Love Dad."

Mom served the nation as well on the home front as a "Rosie the Riveter." She inspected bullets in an ammunition factory in Cumberland, Maryland. At the age of 95, she still displays that determination and grit characteristic of "Rosie the Riveter."

From my earliest memories as a child living on a U.S. Army installation in Zweibrucken, Germany, the military community was filled with camaraderie, fellowship, common objectives and a sense of purpose.

I was blessed to have this type of childhood, and one that was seemingly removed from the social turmoil of the 1960s and 1970s. In our community, I had friends of diverse backgrounds, and we were joined together by a common purpose to defend the nation.

I don't remember my parents loudly proclaiming their patriotism, or making exaggerated claims of heroism about their wartime contributions.

I don't remember them demanding that we join up and serve the nation, as they understood that service could come in many forms.

I don't remember my parents delivering sermons to us about sacrifice.

I do remember that all activities stopped every morning during Reveille and evening Retreat, including moving cars, as the bugler played to honor the nation and sacrifice.

We faced towards the flag, placed our right hands over our hearts, and solemnly stood still.

My parents never had to tell us that it was important to be part of something larger than ourselves.

We just sensed it.

PREFACE

Throughout my life, I have set and pursued ambitious goals that were beyond my sphere of competence. The two subjects embedded in this book, becoming an author and my experience as a military pilot, certainly fall into this category.

As I embarked on these ventures, people wondered if I had a fear of failure.

The short answer is "no." The complicated answer is "yes," but that I'm more fearful of not trying, and then feeling regret in my final years.

This has always been the reason I stomach the risk associated with attempting new, ambitious goals.

I had no idea how to fly a helicopter when I arrived at Fort Rucker, Alabama. I just had faith that I could learn, and as this book will reveal, there were some shaky moments in flight training before I pinned on those silver wings. The outcome was not certain.

Some people view this as confidence, but it is better described as comparative fear.

To most "successful people", the fear of not pursuing worthy goals, is much stronger than the fear of failure. I hope this book encourages readers to move beyond their comfort zone, and pursue their dreams wholeheartedly.

Teddy Roosevelt's quote, "The Man In The Arena", from his April 23, 1910 "Citizenship In A Republic" speech in Paris has always been my battle cry, and ends with the phrase:

"…if he fails, at least he fails while daring greatly, so that his place shall never be with those cold and timid souls who neither know victory nor defeat!"

Frank Van Buren
February 11, 2019

Introduction

The overriding lesson in this book is that peak learning occurs during moments of adversity. If you can recognize this truth and develop fortitude, you will be able to embrace your challenges and persevere through tribulations to reach your full potential.

I believe the most influential lessons of my life have occurred in moments initially deemed as "negative". In retrospect, I now view them as empowering because the adversity forced me to clarify my principles and priorities and to summon the strength, courage, and tenacity to fight on and conquer.

"Life Lessons From The Cockpit" is about learning, and based on the truth above, the majority of the stories do not discuss triumphant moments of celebration and perfect execution. In my opinion, those anecdotes would be better suited for a separate book.

To achieve the goal of writing a genuine book about my personal experiences of learning and growth, it required me to expose my mistakes, challenges and failures. If I did not, the book would not have the integrity that I sought.

The age-old method of military instruction assumes the principles of growth through adversity, and trial-by-fire. Please understand that I am not referring to abusive training, as the leaders whom I served with in the military had an amazing level of concern for their troops. I am simply referring to the concept of encouraging trainees to expand their mental, physical and emotional capacities. You have heard the slogan, "Be All That You Can Be!"

My experiences as a U.S. Army helicopter pilot are recounted throughout the book, especially in flight training when the learning curve was very steep.

My first Instructor Pilot at Fort Rucker was Mr. Dennis Thorp (RIP), a flamboyant character who had forged his aviator skills in Vietnam. Throughout my time under his instruction, I never felt comfortable with my proficiency in the required tasks. The discomfort is encapsulated in this example below of our daily routine.

Instead of riding the bus everyday, "Swanny" (my stick buddy) and I would walk out to the aircraft in the hot Alabama sun with Mr. Thorp. It was his choice, and he was very sociable along the way. Upon arrival at the bird, Thorp would smile and warmly direct us to begin the time consuming pre-flight duties.

Meanwhile, he would daintily put on his gloves while he whistled a happy song, and methodically buckled himself into the aircraft. When he was ready, Mr. Thorp would lean out the window, smile and declare, "You two are going to make us late."

As the scurrying to finish the pre-flight inspection in the hot sun got us worked up into a nice sweat, Thorp would call out the first victim's name.

"Van Buren! You are flying first..." "Yes, Sir!" was my answer, but I murmured, "ah crap".

Swanny breathed a sigh of relief. Both students preferred to fly second because the lucky one could sit in the back seat, get settled down, and watch his stick buddy unravel before getting in the hot seat.

"What is taking you so long to finish?" Thorp would say with a very puzzled look on his face.

As I rushed to climb into the front seat and place my helmet and gloves on, he would blankly stare, then giggle and start the engines before I was ready.

With a wry smile on his face, he would ask why I had not yet called the tower for taxi clearance and departure information. At that point, I was drenched in sweat triggered by the last ten minutes of exertion, the greenhouse effect of the cockpit, and the anxiety induced by this dude's crazy-like-a-clown happiness.

I could feel his glare and it caused immediate stress as I fumbled with the radios to dial in the right frequency to make the call to the tower. I made the radio call, but my cracking voice betrayed my fake composure. It was usually at that moment when Thorp would direct me to pick up the helicopter into a hover, rotor blades turning at full power, and hold it between two other student-piloted helicopters, with blades at full power. This was exceedingly difficult at this stage of proficiency.

"Sir, is there enough room to do that?"

"Candidate, let's go," was his calm, but slightly annoyed response.

It was completely nerve-wracking, and although I tried to look cool, I was scared that I would drift into another helicopter and kill us all. However, I manipulated the controls and the bird rose to about 5 feet off the ground. The powerful thumping of the rotor blades, and the deafening sound caused my body to shudder.

After struggling to hold the hover there for a few long seconds, we would start our taxi out to the runway to depart. Only five minutes into the so-called "flight," and I was already frazzled and filled with self-doubt.

Oh my.

This was not what I expected when I signed up to become a glamorous flyboy! However, it was the training system that would eventually develop a pilot that the Army believed was capable of commanding a Blackhawk during a tactical night flight with soldiers onboard.

After a year of trying to keep up with the endless challenges and constant stress, I walked across a beautiful stage in the U.S. Army Aviation Museum and was awarded my silver Aviator Wings. My mother pinned them on me, and it was a sweet victory!

Throughout the flight school journey, I never felt highly confident in my flight proficiency.

It wasn't until about a year later when I experienced an engine failure in the rugged mountains of Honduras, did I recognize the merit in the military training system. It was my ability to calmly function with con-fidence under pressure, a core tenant of flight instruc-tors like Dennis Thorp that saved our lives.

The anecdotes discussed in this book are not glamor-ous war stories told to impress the reader. However, they are stories filled with disabling emotions that I had to overcome in order to succeed, such as indif-ference, fear, comfort, disappointment, pride, and in-security. It is the wrestling with these mental states that make these stories fantastic teaching tools forever burned into my soul.

I hope you will benefit from reading about my pow-erful lessons as a Blackhawk Pilot, because I believe if you are reading this book, we must share the desire for self-improvement and a fulfilling life.

Opportunity Wears Camouflage

My parents never pushed us to serve the nation, but during my first year (1984) at Shippensburg University of Pennsylvania, I decided to join ROTC and prepare for a military career.

Additionally, I played inter-collegiate football. In the first three years, I earned All-Conference and Honorable Mention All-American football honors. Although I was playing at a Division II school, I was making plans to play in the NFL, in whatever capacity possible.

However, in the fall of my junior year, I sustained a major knee injury that changed the course of my life. My initial thoughts as I lay in the hospital bed were dismal, but in time, I understood that it was one of my finest moments.

This catastrophic injury to my left knee forced me to undergo a grueling personal journey of rehabilitation that ultimately demonstrated my ability to overcome adversity, and inspire my teammates. I was named team captain and awarded the "Ray Ellis Fighting Heart" award.

A sweet personal victory had arisen out of the adversity and I was empowered, but the dream of playing in the NFL had gone awry.

With the NFL dream fading as fast as my 40-yard dash time, I began to focus on a military career. Although I had overcome the challenge of the extensive knee surgery, the rehabilitation delayed my scheduled U.S. Army ROTC training and officer commissioning ceremony.

So after college graduation, I attended the required officer training at Fort Bragg about a year behind my peer group. The highlight of the training was an exhilarating ride in the back of a UH-60 Blackhawk helicopter, skimming along the treetops!

That moment was electric, and one that would change my life. I knew that I wanted to serve my country, but my desire to become a pilot rose exponentially after the experience. I resolved to find a way to squeeze into flight training, although it was a long shot so late in the process.

Upon completion of the officer training, I received my Second Lieutenant commission, with orders to follow at a later date. I was soon to learn that my dream of jumping off that helicopter ride and heading directly to flight training at Fort Rucker, Alabama was not going to happen. The highly sought-after slots had already been allocated to my peers.

Shortly after returning home to Maryland as a young officer, my father passed away and was buried with full military honors at Arlington National Cemetery. His passing and burial heightened my sense of urgency and impatience to get on active duty and to become a pilot.

In the transition period, I lived with my mom on her couch and found a job with the Harris/3M Corporation selling fax machines door to door on 100% commission. I also began attending Maryland National Guard Duty as a Second Lieutenant, while lobbying the Military Personnel Center for a ticket to flight training. "No chance anytime soon," was the common refrain.

I did manage to join a National Guard helicopter unit, but there were no promises of receiving a flight school spot. The aviators in that unit were very nice and professional and would allow me to ride along on occasion.

I deeply wanted to become a helicopter pilot, but it was clear that I had missed the window of opportunity in the traditional process, due solely to the college football knee injury.

The frustration and helplessness grew after learning that this unit also had a long backlog of "wanna-be" aviators. We were clearly identified because of the lack of flight suits and silver wings, and the bad habit of complaining to each other about our low-value positions in the unit and the long waiting period before we went to flight school.

I guess we should have been nicknamed the "penguins." Birds that just could not fly. It was a miserable group!

One day, I walked into a building in Herndon, Virginia in my business suit and tie trying to find a buyer of a new fax machine. Instead, I bumped into Don Hess, a retired Chief Warrant Officer CW5, and Executive Director of the U.S. Army Warrant Officers Association. In the U.S. Army, the majority of the pilots are Warrant Officers, who receive officer status in exchange for technical expertise in a specialty such as aviation.

What started out as a pitch to sell Mr. Hess a fax machine, turned into a one-hour discussion about the military. We really connected on a personal level because we both seemed to have a genuine interest in learning about the other.

I learned that Don Hess was an experienced officer with service in Vietnam. I told Mr. Hess about my goal to become a pilot, and my discouragement because my National Guard unit was full of young officers waiting (ahead of me) for a flight school date.

He surprised me and suggested that if I truly wanted to become an active duty pilot, there was another option through the Warrant Officer Flight Training program, but that the path would carry risks. He had worked in Vietnam with a pilot who was now the Commanding General at Recruiting Command, and said he would look into it for me.

I was energized, because I had stumbled into an enabler, and possibly a connector. I was able to powerfully and genuinely articulate my goals and vision, and he sensed that I was a committed young man.

Mr. Hess talked to the General and then told me that there was clear path, but it had a rub. I would have to resign my Second Lieutenant commission and enter into active duty as a much lower E-3 rank (Private First Class), with a direct assignment to Warrant Officer Candidate School. If I made it through the first 6 weeks of WOCS, I would immediately begin flight training to become an aviator.

Mr. Hess also explained the downside of this unconventional path. If I "washed-out" of flight training, I would have permanently forfeited my officer status and would be required to serve three years beginning as a Private First Class doing whatever the U.S. Army needed. However, if I made it through the training, I would be assigned to fly the best aircraft in the Army's fleet.

It was risky, but I immediately leapt at the chance because I was committed to becoming a pilot. I was much more impatient and risk tolerant than my group of wingless peers. They were astounded when I shared my plan to make it to flight school, and most of them thought that I was crazy or stupid (maybe both).

I didn't care. I was all-in. This was my opportunity.

So in 1989, I resigned my commission, entered into the active duty in the U.S. Army as a Private First Class, and headed to Fort Rucker to become a pilot. When the TAC (Training Assistance Counseling) Officers learned my story, they decided to give me special attention, but it didn't bother me at all. I was 23 years old, and running down a dream.

Over the next six years, I served honorably and proudly as a UH-60 Blackhawk pilot stationed throughout Central America, Europe, the Middle East, and the USA, flying a variety of difficult missions on behalf of our nation.

What was the lesson I learned from this episode of my life?

Opportunity is often camouflaged, and it rarely presents itself in an ideal manner.

Look for the crack in the door, and when you see it, boldly and courageously run through it.

Expect Obstacles

It was 4:30 am when we boarded the white bus to the Military Entrance Processing Station. "MEPS" is where applicants for military service go to complete the enlistment process. Since I resigned my commission as an officer in order to get to flight school, I had to re-enlist and go through the standard process.

After going through a security screening and completing the paperwork, I began the comprehensive medical examination. At that point, I would have never guessed the rest of the day was going to be so stressful.

I did fine on the vision and general exam, but the train started to come off the tracks when I walked into the hearing section. As I sat in a chair, the young medical assistant began to fit me for proper hearing protection.

She firmly pushed the orange plug deep into my right ear that jammed excess wax down into its channel and significantly degraded my hearing.

I looked up at her with a puzzled look on my face, my palms open, and said, "You just clogged my ear!"

Her nonchalant response made it evident to me that she didn't care about the gravity of my problem. MEPS was the last gate I had to pass through before heading for Fort Rucker, Alabama, home of U.S. Army Aviation.

I was very annoyed and asked her to document the problem so I could appeal the results later if I failed the hearing test. She gave me a carefree shrug and directed me to step into the hearing booth to perform the test.

I was stressed because if I failed this simple hearing test, even after passing the comprehensive flight physical a month earlier, I would still be disqualified from service and my dream would die.

Once I received her instructions, I quickly figured out a strategy to improve my chances for success with the clogged ear. As the repetitive sound (beep-beep-beep) began to trail off to the point of silence, I was instructed to let up on the handheld button.

So with the right ear, I continued to push the button for an additional few seconds after I heard the final beeps trailing off into silence. With every frequency, I held that button longer than I actually heard the sound, and I prayed it would work. When I walked out of the sound booth, she told me that I was "Good-to-Go", a military motivational slogan.

Good gracious. I almost felt like celebrating, but I still had to get through the orthopedic section, and I knew that my knee injury was going to be an obstacle.

Although I had demonstrated the resilience of the knee throughout an entire season of college football, the MEPS orthopedic doctor had a different set of standards. He was considering whether the U.S. Army should invest $1 million just to get me through initial training, and multiple millions to keep me in the air for my six-year commitment.

The doctor went through the standard orthopedic examination without making many comments but hesitated as he eyed the long, surgical scars on my left knee.

He walked over and picked up my medical file, and read it for a few minutes in silence. I began to worry when he decided to seek a few more opinions on my medical qualifications for flight training.

When he excused himself and walked out of the room, I got a sinking feeling in my stomach that I was about to be tested, so I mentally prepared myself. The doctor and two others walked back into the room and began to ask me general questions about the knee.

"Private Van Buren, how does your knee feel?"

I responded with as much confidence and enthusiasm as I could muster.

"Sir, it feels great. I played a full year of college football after the knee injury, and never missed a workout. If you look at my files, there are letters of support written by my surgeon and the Director of Athletic Training at Shippensburg University, Steve Heckler. I am fit to fight."

The three doctors then asked me to get into a full squat position, and walk like a duck to the other side of the room.

"No problem, sir," I said with a calm, self-assured voice.

It was extremely painful due to the poor range of motion caused by the scar tissue. Regardless, I had to continue on and focus on making it to the other side of the room.

When I got close to the wall, I heard a voice directing me to continue back, as the scrutinizing doctors requested another lap. Everything was on the line for me, and this required showing a poker face and removing any doubt about my tenacity or readiness to serve.

The three doctors huddled around and whispered for a few moments before one said, "OK, Private Van Buren, you are Good-To-Go."

Sometimes, you just have to project confidence and enthusiasm, even if you don't feel that way. The doctors' decision was influenced by my positive, can-do attitude, and that may have saved me that day.

What a relief! I had successfully made it through Day 1, but I sensed that it was not going to be smooth sailing on this journey. If I wanted to achieve my goals, I would have to surmount many obstacles.

As I boarded the white bus to head out of MEPS, I thought of the lyrics to the 1960s song by The Shirelles: "Mama said there'll be days like this."

As the bus drove off, I had a smile on my face and felt relieved because I made it through the process. I was finally on my way to Fort Rucker, and quietly singing the words of Tom Petty's classic tune, "Runnin down a dream."

> "Yeah, runnin' down a dream
> Never would come to me
> Workin' on a mystery
> Goin' wherever it leads
> I'm runnin' down a dream"

Find Things In Common

Our TAC Officers loved to wake us up at 4:30 am by throwing steel trash cans onto the old barracks' linoleum floors. It was a painful way to wake up, hearing the sound of that steel trash can bouncing down the center aisle between the rows of beds.

Training Advisory and Counseling officers were responsible for the initial preparation of the candidates who would become Warrant Officers after their technical training. For aviation types, that was flight school. It was an opportunity for the U.S. Army to filter out weak candidates before the flight training began. This six-week period was called Warrant Officer Candidates School, or WOCS.

During the program, we did lots of academics, cleaning, inspections and anything else the TAC Officers could dream up, just to test our commitment to becoming a pilot. However, their favorite was PT or physical training. They loved to "smoke us" in the early morning.

The guys in charge of the filtering system for Class 90-14 were Chief Warrant Officers Cosby and Paul. These officers were very different, but they made one heck of a team.

Mr. Cosby was a brash, aggressive logistics guy who I imagine would be very good running a FedEx warehouse. Mr. Paul was a quiet, serious aviator who had a personality that reminded me of Clint Eastwood in Dirty Harry. Cosby was loud and Paul was soft spoken. Cosby was black, and Paul was white. Fire and Ice.

Mr. Cosby used to entertain himself by turning his office into "Mr. Cosby's Game Room." To enter his office, I had to knock on his door, and declare, "Sir, Candidate Van Buren requests permission to enter the game room, Sir!"

He would yell out, "Candidate Van Buren, Enter!"

I'd toss a quarter into his office, and run in and begin a smoke session filled with every exercise he wanted to see. The entering candidate was "his game."

Mr. Paul preferred to make candidates brace against the wall, which is a stance that requires three points of contact: Head, butt, and heels. Then he would stand in front of the candidates and just quietly look right through them with the Clint Eastwood look.

The class was filled with candidates from all walks of life, and all geographic regions of the country: Kent Walker, Paul Schlett, Bernie Smith, Jose Madrietta, Bob Piselli, Matt Weller, John Ramiccio, Chris Jackson, Ken

Denby, Gene Jarvis, John Nailor, Jim Dwyer, to name a few. They were all smart, patriotic and brave Americans.

It did not take long after arrival before this diverse set of candidates began to find common bonds, interests, and experiences. We all had shaved heads, wore the same green and olive drab colored uniforms, and had the same dream to become pilots. The TAC Officers understood that a common nemesis is also an effective way to create cohesiveness.

After the jarringly loud wake-up from the hurled trash cans, Mr. Cosby would stroll into the center of the barracks, and start screaming that everyone needed to be outside in five minutes in their PT gear, after preparing our beds and lockers for inspection. We were going to do a "little run."

We jumped up and scrambled like cockroaches when the light was turned on. We were bumping into each other, and racing into the bathroom before the fun run. It was a chaotic mess.

Within five minutes of the painful wake-up, the formation took off into the dark at a brisk pace. One candidate would jump out front and lead the Jodies, military slang for cadence calls. Mr. Paul liked to push the pace, and get the smoke session started quickly. Whenever some of the formation would start to fall behind, the

TAC Officers would stop everyone and have a smoke session in the grass.

By the time we returned from the run, our clothes were drenched in sweat and our chests were burning. Then the real fun started.

"I want you to be back down here in five minutes ready for inspections in your Class A (suits & ties) uniforms, shaved and showered. And make sure your locker is inspection ready, boots shined, clothes folded. GO!" Cosby would scream.

Of course, this was virtually impossible to accomplish, yet initially we were foolish enough to believe that we could do it. We all ran back inside and tried to change out of our dripping wet workout gear into suit & ties, within five minutes. No way.

Some candidates figured out how to cut corners by having their gear pre-positioned the night before, so they may have made it back downstairs within the five minutes. As they trickled into the formation area without the entire unit, the TAC Officers would go bananas and put them in a "front leaning rest" position (push-up). It became very clear that if the unit split up because of individual selfishness, then that would trigger another smoke session.

Eventually, we decided to work as a team to complete the preparations and tasks inside of the barracks, then we walked out as one unit together, even if we were fifteen minutes late.

Bingo.

Chiefs Paul and Cosby rejoiced because we finally got it. Their objective was to teach us, through pain and frustration, how to work quickly and effectively as a team.

The military does a fantastic job of eliminating the artificial barriers that society creates, by instilling a common purpose with common experiences. This can be replicated with any team in the civilian sector through effective leadership and team-based incentive programs.

Recently on the trading floor in Charlotte, North Carolina, I was in a giddy mood after a profitable bond trade and decided to celebrate by singing a little "happy" song.

I don't know why, since it has been over 23 years since I departed the military, but I picked a classic Army "Jody" called "A Yellow Bird".

With a smile on my face, I started singing out loud...

"A yellow bird, With a yellow bill..."

Next to me was a team member named Casey Carroll, a former U.S. Army Ranger who was eleven years old when I got out of the service in 1996. We trained at different installations, never served in the same unit, and had vastly different jobs in the military.

As I proceeded with the "Jody", Casey continued to look at his computer screen, but smiled and immediately joined in the Jody without missing a beat...

"A yellow bird, With a yellow bill, Was sittin' on, My window sill, I lured him in, With a peace of bread, And then I smashed his little head!"

It was hilarious, and we laughed for a few minutes, amazed that one silly song could bridge the generation gap of two veterans who happened to be working next to each other.

We both understood at that very moment, the power of a common experience.

It reminded me of the importance of bridging differences between human beings, and how simple it can be to find common bonds if we just focus on learning more about the people we meet at work or in social situations.

Historically, the military has been a leader in creating highly functioning teams, formed with members from all walks of life. This includes demographic diversity, but also people from urban, rural and suburban upbringings, and the spectrum of social-economic groups.

They do it by creating a common experience, usually basic training, which is the first place where the Jodies are used to instill a sense of camaraderie and esprit de corps.

When you sing a Jody, it connects you to the unit, fortifies the soul, and helps a soldier to tolerate physical and mental hardship. It unites, and inspires the collective group to go further than the individual members. The foundation is solidified by a common overarching purpose, to defend the nation.

When Casey effortlessly joined me in this silly Jody, it highlighted a common bond. So, how can individuals and civilian organizations replicate the military's proven formula for building bonds represented in this chapter?

Demonstrate a genuine interest in learning about the people you come in contact with, beyond the specific reason for your engagement. Inquire about their childhood, current interests and activities. Inquire about the family, and share your information.

The questions may vary, but the intent is to identify common bonds and experiences.

EMBRACE DISCOMFORT

There I was, in the spring of 1990, at the U.S. Army's Flight Training Center in Fort Rucker, Alabama. It was over 100 degrees inside the cockpit of the green UH-1 Huey helicopter, and it was about to get hotter. The old Vietnam era Huey, painted with orange doors to alert everyone to the danger of a student pilot, was loud, rough and intimidating.

The most elementary maneuver for a helicopter pilot trainee to learn is how to hover. Hovering is when the helicopter is flown so that it maintains a constant position over the ground, and it requires the student to multitask. Helicopter pilots refer to this coordination of hand and feet movements as "inherent control coupling."

I was sitting in the left front seat, sweating profusely in my green Nomex flight suit and helmet, gloves and combat boots. In the cockpit seat to the right of me was Mr. Thorp, my longhaired instructor pilot who wore Ray-ban sunglasses, even when the sun was not shining. My stick buddy named Swanny was observing from the back "jump seat."

As mentioned earlier, Mr. Thorp was one of the veteran retired aviators with combat experience in Vietnam that the army hired as contractors. Their job was to teach the dangerous first phase of helicopter training to a bunch of "wanna-be" aviators, right out of basic officer training. The job required immense aviator skills, confidence and vigilance.

In addition to being an excellent pilot, Mr. Thorp was sarcastic and loved to rattle his students with harmless "head games." One of his favorite tactics with me was to comment on the crookedness of my teeth as I struggled to fly.

I could feel his stare, and then he would politely ask, "Frank, I don't get it. Why didn't your parents get braces for you? My goodness, your teeth are crooked!"

The mental stress applied was part of the Army's proven process to develop aviators to the required proficiency level before receiving the silver wings at graduation and being sent out to active duty units.

"OK, Frank, the goal today is to hover the helicopter on your own. I am going to give you just one of the three controls to the aircraft, the anti-torque pedals." he calmly stated as the helicopter hovered perfectly with apparently no effort required on his part. It was like watching a duck glide across a pond.

"All you have to do is keep the aircraft pointed at that large tree in the distance. It is very simple, Frank. You have the pedals."

"Yes sir, I have the pedals."

The pedals on the helicopter control the yaw of the aircraft. The yawing movement is when the helicopter's heading is changed by rotating the nose to one side or the other around the vertical axis, using the anti-torque control provided by the small tail rotor. If a helicopter ever loses this anti-torque capability, it violently spins around like a top.

In no time at all, the aircraft's nose was turning away from the distant tree to the right, requiring an input of left pedal to bring it back. I pushed the left pedal, but far too hard, causing the nose to whip back around past the tree and too far left.

"Candidate Van Buren, what are you doing? Easy on the pedals."

"Yes, sir."

I pushed the right pedal...and passed the tree again. Then left pedal...passed the tree again. Back and forth I went, with the frustrated sighs of Dennis Thorp filling my ears. This seemingly simple task, analogous to finding the sweet spot when learning to manage the clutch in a stick-shifted car, introduced major stress into my life!

Finally, I settled the aircraft down and pretty much kept the nose pointed towards the tree over 100 yards away.

"OK, Frank. That is good enough. I have the pedals."

"Yes sir, you have the pedals." I said as I took a deep breath and began to realize that this year was going to be a bit more difficult than I had imagined back home.

"Candidate Van Buren, I will keep all controls except for the cyclic stick," he stated over the incredibly distracting noise of the helicopter. "All you have to do now is keep the aircraft level. You have the cyclic."

"Yes sir, I have the cyclic."

The cyclic stick is connected to the floor and located between the pilot's legs. The control is called the cyclic because it changes the pitch angle of the rotor blades cyclically. The result is to tilt the rotor disk in a particular direction, resulting in the helicopter moving in that direction. If the pilot pushes the cyclic forward, for example, the rotor disk tilts forward, and the rotor produces a thrust vector in the forward direction.

It didn't take but a second for the amazingly stable aircraft piloted by Mr. Thorp to begin to move forward. At that point, I pulled back on the cyclic (too abruptly) and the nose arched back like a bucking horse, and we moved rapidly backward.

"Whoa, whoa, whoa! Easy cowboy!" Mr. Thorp yelled over the intercom. "Just nice and gradual!"

I continued this over correcting dance for ten minutes, with him literally saving us from crashing, and I was already tired. Finally, I managed to settle down the bucking bronco to his satisfaction.

"OK, that is enough Van Buren. I have the cyclic," the salty instructor said.

I relinquished the controls, however, I felt by the tone of his voice that I was not performing up to his expectations.

"Finally, I am going to give you the last control, the collective stick. All you have to do is to keep the helicopter hovering at ten feet above the ground. I will keep all the other controls. You have the collective." he calmly informed me with a huge "cat that ate the canary" grin on his grizzled face.

The collective pitch control or collective lever is normally located on the left side of the pilot's seat. The collective changes the pitch angle of all the main rotor blades collectively (i.e., all at the same time), and controls the climb and descent movement of the aircraft.

"I have the collective," I quietly said with a bit of trepidation in my voice.

Off we went. Up from 10 feet to about 30, as I had too much power applied through the raised collective.

"Like a rocket ship, eh Frankie?" I think he enjoyed the fun.

So I pushed it down...too much, and we dropped towards the ground rapidly.

"I have the controls!" he screamed as he faked outrage at my apparent attempt to actually try to kill him.

Then he gave the collective back, and let me play the elevator game for several minutes before holding it steady.

"That's decent, Frank!"

"Thank you, sir."

"Now before we head back for the day, I want you to take all the controls, and hover this aircraft", he commanded, with the knowledge that he should stay alert so I didn't get us both killed.

I took the controls, and attempted to hover with all three controls...and it was a disaster of an attempt.

Up too high, then down too fast only to barely save us from crashing, nose too far left, and the helicopter banked hard right...it was quite a ride. I think I heard that old bird Thorp laughing loudly over the roar of the engines and the whop-whop of the blades. He was clearly enjoying this spectacle.

"Well, that is enough. I have the controls," he said with disgust dripping from his tone. "That was one of the ugliest displays of hovering that I have ever witnessed. We are going to have to work on your ability to do more than one thing at a time."

Somehow, ten hours of flight training later, I figured out how to hold a solid hover. I had a great deal of respect and gratitude to ole' Dennis Thorp for keeping me out of the grave during these precarious early days.

The uncomfortable experience of learning how to hover is symbolic of the challenge that any of us undergoes when transitioning from a job/career/life of competence to a new endeavor. It can be downright exhausting; mentally, emotionally and physically.

However, we will never grow and reach our ambitious goals if we do not put ourselves in uncomfortable and challenging scenarios.

Just understand that the discomfort is temporary in nature, and it will be mitigated by the proud and rewarding moment when you accomplish your ambitious goals!

Recognize A Bad Fit

There I was, at Fort Rucker Alabama, riding in the back seat of a green Huey helicopter watching my stick buddy Swanny struggle to fly straight and level at 2,000 feet.

On paper, Swanny was the ideal candidate. He was confident, smart, well respected, and had scored high on the flight aptitude test. On top of that, he was tall, handsome and articulate. Before flight training started, most of my fellow student pilots believed that Swanny would easily earn his wings and thrive as a helicopter pilot for years to come. It didn't turn out that way...

Our instructor, Mr. Dennis Thorp, sat in the right seat of the aircraft and slyly leaned over and placed Swanny's radio switches in the mute position so he could not hear outside communication.

I knew what was coming next, but Swanny did not... the dreaded "autorotation."

The maneuver is important because it is the primary emergency procedure that a helicopter pilot uses to deal with a dangerous engine failure. The autorotation is one heck of a scary flight maneuver to learn because ole' Mr. Thorp never warned us that it was coming. As the student observing from the back seat, I had the luxury of preparing for the impending maneuver.

In normal flight, the engine turns the rotors (blades) through the air. The blades are placed in an "angle of attack" that causes a pressure differential, thereby creating lift. When the engine fails, there is no longer sufficient power to keep the rotors turning.

The required response is for the pilot to immediately enter into a steep descent to encourage airflow through the rotors, which keeps them turning.

The "potential energy" in the form of altitude, is traded for the "kinetic energy" of the spinning rotors. When the rapidly descending aircraft gets close to the ground, the pilot reintroduces the pitch angle into the rotors using the flight controls, and creates just enough temporary lift to slow the descent and safely land.

Whew!

So after Mr. Thorp covertly turned down Swanny's radios, he made the obligatory call to the tower with our exact location, just in case we crashed and needed assistance.

"Cairns Tower, this is Instructor 3-0, at training location 1-2, entering into a simulated engine failure."

At that moment I gritted my teeth and braced, as Mr. Thorp announced the surprise (simulated) engine failure by literally "rolling down the throttle" (reducing power) to the point where actual flight at that altitude was unsustainable. Swanny was alerted by the jarringly loud "Low RPM" alarm, and the cockpit illuminated with flashing lights similar to a decorated Christmas tree.

At that very moment, Swanny was supposed to take immediate action with the flight controls and enter into a steep descent that resembled a roller coaster drop at Six Flags Texas. After the harrowing drop, Swanny was required to identify a suitable landing area, analyze critical data like engine temperature and pressure, and overcome a basic instinct to tighten the muscles, close the eyes and whimper "mama!"

But with Swanny, there was one little problem...

Swanny hated "that" feeling in the stomach, so his unintentional reaction was to literally let go of the flight controls and scream. No joke. He screamed.

It was ugly and harrowing because from my perch in the back seat, I could see the rotor blades slowing down to the speed that converted the aircraft into a falling heavy rock, and eventually a simmering spot in some farmer's field.

"Good Lord, this freakin' dude is going to kill us". I murmured under my breath.

The salty Instructor, Dennis Thorp glared at Swanny for a couple of seconds with disgust in his face, then he angrily seized the controls, and dove the aircraft toward the ground in a recovery maneuver that I am sure he learned flying combat missions in Vietnam.

As soon as Mr. Thorp got the aircraft back into a safe mode of flight, he looked over at Swanny and said, "You have the controls."

With his face flushed and voice quiet like a mouse, Swanny began his climb back to altitude, while Thorp shook his head, and stared at him.

Upon reaching altitude and allowing Swanny to get comfortably back into his rhythm of flying straight and level again, ole' Thorp called back to the tower, and the fun resumed.

"Ugh! Here we go again...this is so painful", I thought.

"Simulated engine failure!" Thorp announced as the throttle power was reduced, and the blades again slowed down with the accompanying flashing lights and very annoying horn.

Swanny again repeated his actions, and I experienced the same sense of helplessness and anxiety sitting in the back seat along for the "joy ride." After multiple episodes of this terrifying "ride along", Swanny eventually informed Thorp that he had to puke.

"Holy cow," I thought.

That was usually when a very frustrated Mr. Thorp fired off a few choice words and placed the aircraft in a steep rolling dive down to the beautiful Alabama countryside.

Now I thought I was going to puke.

Upon landing, Swanny opened the door and proceeded to lose his breakfast, while steam could be seen emitting from Thorp's helmet.

After Swanny finished, he took the controls back, and we climbed back up for more of this fantastic fun. I couldn't wait until it was my turn to entertain ole' Thorp.

Well, Swanny "washed out" of flight training a few weeks later, and began the next phase of his life.

Sometimes, a person just isn't suited for a particular job. No matter how hard he tried, or how many chances he was given, it simply was a bad fit.

However, Swanny had many fine attributes that would apply very well in a different line of work, so I bet he did well in life anyway.

Unlike Swanny's situation that resulted in a rapid change, most people slowly realize they are not suited for, inspired by, or fulfilling their true potential as they drift deeper into a career.

The signs are always there, but the eagerness and pride of embarking on a new career path usually mask the truth. Over time, one becomes content with an acceptable level of discontent, and the inertia of life makes it easier to safely continue on rather than initiate a risky life change.

It is far better to make a change early on in an endeavor if you recognize that the path is not suited for you.

We only have a limited amount of time on this earth, so it should be spent pursuing worthy goals consistent with our natural attributes, values and genuine interests.

LEAVE THE NEST

Somewhere around the sixth or seventh week of Army flight training, a few weeks after my stick buddy "Swanny" had washed out, Instructor Dennis Thorp was putting me through some basic flight maneuvers at one of Fort Rucker's stage fields. The fourteen stage fields account for over 2,000 acres of land in southeastern Alabama and serve as the main helicopter pilot training areas.

I landed the green helicopter with orange doors (alerting the world that a dangerous student pilot is training) on the runway after completing several patterns around the stage field. I was still shaky on the controls and felt like I was one mistake away from the grave, if not for Mr. Thorp's daily supervision. By no means did I feel confident enough for what was about to happen next...

Mr. Thorp, who sat in the right seat of the aircraft, looked over and said to me, "Candidate Van Buren, I think you are ready to do your solo ride. I'm going to get out, and you are going to complete three trips around the stage field flight pattern."

A wave of anxiety rushed over me, even though I knew the solo ride would happen within this two-week period. He made a call to the control tower to inform them of my impending solo ride, gave me a few final tips, wished me good luck, and then disconnected his audio cord and got out.

Yup, he just got out. Thorp walked off to the side of the runway, turned around, and had the nerve to smile and wave!

"Good gracious, I'm on my own!"

So that is how the Army cuts the umbilical cord. Abruptly!

I gathered myself with a positive affirmation, took a few deep breaths, and made a call to the control tower to announce my intention to take-off and fly my first lap.

"Tower, this is Thirteen Kilo, on runway 36, ready for departure", I said with anxiety betraying my voice.

The tower cleared me for departure, and I applied power and got the bird airborne, made a left turn on departure, and flew the downwind leg of the pattern. So far, it all was going well. I made the call to the tower announcing my left turns on to base leg, then final approach, and was cleared to land.

The first approach was downright ugly. I came in too high and fast, and the air traffic controller must have recognized it. "Thirteen Kilo, slow your approach!"

"Tower, Thirteen Kilo, roger that." I replied. In response, I pulled back aggressively on the cyclic stick to slow down, and the aircraft's nose pitched up, and I started to sink quickly. I recovered by adding power in an abrupt manner and somehow got the beast landed on the ground. Whew!

I looked over at ole' Thorp, and he was just staring at me blankly. He must have been wondering how this was going to end, but there was nothing he could do to help me. The salty instructor knew that it was an important moment for his student to struggle, and grow.

The second and third trips around the stage field were equally ugly but in creative ways. Somehow, I managed to fly the aircraft around that stage field by myself three times without getting myself killed.

Halleluiah. It was a nerve racking and uncomfortable experience, but I was simply thankful that I made it.

Mr. Thorp shook his head with disappointment the whole walk back to the aircraft. He climbed into the cockpit, connected his audio cord, looked at me and just giggled. Then, I laughed. It was clear that he did not appreciate my undeveloped aviator skills, but he was satisfied that I had reached this milestone.

"Congratulations. Let's head back home".

Within another week, after the last student completed their solo ride, Class 90-14 celebrated with a ritual that goes back to 1970 and is part of Army Aviation tradition: The Solo Cycle.

All of the flight students lined up on both sides of the street near the barracks, and the last person in our class to solo, Chris Jackson, rode a decorated bicycle dubbed the "Solo Cycle", through a gauntlet of water balloons.

Chris was not the traditional type of student to solo last in a class, one that has struggled. Instead, he was a highly competent commercial airline pilot, but the instructors decided it made for a nice joke.

Happiness was in the air, because the class had completed a significant psychological milestone, flying alone, and we were ready to advance to the next phase of training. Each student was better off for enduring the discomfort of this harrowing "solo ride" on the journey to achieving our aviator's wings.

Similar to completing a solo ride, most people have significant moments, early in life, when their decision to engage in a new uncomfortable process made them a better person.

Maybe it was the first time you were "home alone" as a child?

Maybe it was the first time you drove without anyone else in the car?

Maybe it was the moment when your parents drove away from the freshman college dorm?

Maybe it had to do with overcoming an athletic weakness, spiritual bankruptcy, a non-productive relationship, academic challenges, intense military training or career obstacles?

It is clear that to experience significant growth; you must be willing to go through the process of "growing pains." The benefit of the experience is usually obvious over time. This is one of the essential ingredients of every successful human story.

If you want to accomplish meaningful long-term goals, you must be willing to leave the safety of the nest, and endure short-term discomfort.

GET BACK UP

I was sitting at a table in the briefing room, waiting for the DES Standardization Instructor Pilot ("SIP") to arrive. It was Phase 2 (P2) test day, and I was the first student in the class to face the legendary Instructors.

The Directorate of Evaluation and Standardization is a Department of the Army Field Operating Agency that ensures standardization of Army Aviation operations worldwide, and their SIPs wear a rectangular orange patch on their flight suits. For Quality Control purposes, they don't announce their plans for arrival. Even our normal instructors like Mr. Thorp were not warned of their arrival.

Every Army pilot, even highly seasoned aviators like Mr. Thorp, knows the evolutionary reaction to that Orange patch. It is similar to the quick moment of fear you experience when seeing a snake.

The DES instructors are highly professional and take pride in their role as the guardians of the highest standards of U.S. Army Aviation. Their integrity is beyond reproach.

The P2 check ride is the culmination of the Primary training phase, which teaches students the basics of flying. We had about 50 hours of flight time at that point. The P2 is significant because it was the first test that was conducted by an instructor other than Mr. Thorp.

In retrospect, the fact that I was the first student to be tested for P2 proficiency had less to do with my skills, relative to my peers. All of us were at the same novice level, with the exception of Chris Jackson.

As mentioned in the last chapter, Chris was an active commercial airline pilot who joined the Army reserves to serve the nation and to learn how to fly something new. The rest of us were just trying not to get washed out.

I was a direct witness to Swanny washing out after only 3 weeks of Primary 1 training, so I knew the threat was real. After Swanny departed the program, I sensed that Mr. Thorp was very disappointed that one of his students failed, and he took personal responsibility for the outcome.

Similar to any talented and dedicated teacher, he believed that "there are no bad students, only bad teachers". That sense of responsibility is consistent across all excellent teachers; my 4th-grade teacher Dee Anne Egan, still keeps track of her students on Facebook over 40 years later!

So Thorp placed an extra amount of instruction into getting me prepared to excel in the class. He wanted more than anything for me to succeed, as a reflection of his competence, and I benefitted immensely for it.

Mr. Thorp conducted the P1 check ride, and he signed off on my capabilities with fantastic scores. I was starting to feel good about my aviator skills!

You know where this is going...

When the time came for instructors to advance students to the P2 check ride, Thorp enthusiastically recommended me as the first student to test.

Back to the story...

I could hear footsteps approaching from my rear, so I stood up to greet the SIP. When I turned to extend my hand and the required greeting, I immediately saw that bright orange patch, and it was like Indiana Jones nose-to-nose with a cobra. Yikes!

After exchanging pleasantries and focusing on calming down my breathing, he proceeded with the oral portion of the exam, which tested for knowledge in a wide range of topics including aerodynamics, aero medical, weather and aircraft mechanics and performance.

Although I knew most of the answers, I certainly didn't impress this fellow, who showed absolutely no sense of warmth or interest in knowing me as a human being. He was there to see if I met his standards. No smiles, no wit, no humor. All business.

After the oral exam, we walked out to the flight line, just the two of us. The guy was like the Terminator, and never made one attempt to relax me like the witty, sarcastic and engaging Mr. Thorp. However, I was focused and was also not really interested in small talk.

When we got to the aircraft, he instructed me to get the aircraft pre-flighted, and I was happy to do so. He didn't pull any of Mr. Thorp's antics of applying stress, and instead just quietly observed.

We both got in the aircraft, went through our pre-flight checklist, and I felt like things were going well. I fired up the bird, made my mandatory calls to the tower with confidence, and picked up the bird into a hover to proceed. That was when I heard his icy voice over the intercom.

"Put the helicopter down now."

I complied, although a bit puzzled. He pointed to the back cargo door that was left open and stated in a cool and detached voice.

"You departed without closing the door. That is a violation of safety protocol. You failed the pre-flight portion of the exam."

I almost came undone with anger. I began to explain that I normally had a stick buddy who sits in the back and was responsible for closing the door. I wanted to tell him about everything I did to get here including the knee rehabilitation, the long wait for a flight school slot, the risk I took by resigning my commission! I was absolutely rattled by his indifference.

Then I recognized that he didn't care. It was either a pass or fail. So I unfastened my harness, disconnected from the radios, opened the door and walked around the helicopter and slammed the freakin' door closed.

When I got back in and got strapped back in, he just calmly said: "let's go".

I made the call to the tower, taxied out to the runway, and departed to the training stage field. Along the way, he tested me on many different maneuvers and verbal knowledge, and I seem to be doing ok, although I could not erase the negative thought about that crazy open door violation!

We arrived at the stage field traffic pattern and were on the downwind leg when he rolled down the throttle (power) on the UH-1 Huey and totally surprised me with a simulated engine failure. Blood pressure went up!

The cockpit lit up like a Christmas tree with flashing red lights, audio horn blared in my helmet, and I had to immediately take action!

I quickly lowered the collective stick in my left hand, which initiated a steep drop from altitude necessary to drive airflow through the powerless rotor blades, and I got the aircraft under control. I began to bark out the necessary data, including airspeed, RPM, rate of descent, engine oil temperature and pressure.

I eyed the runway for a maneuver called a "180-Degree Autorotation". This maneuver is used to safely maneuver the helicopter after an engine failure to a suitable landing area that is behind you.

As we were descending rapidly from altitude, I started my right 180-degree turn. The objective is to roll out of the turn, get the aircraft aligned with the runway prior to descending through 200 feet. If this is not the case, the Instructor Pilot will abort the maneuver and take the controls back from the student.

Ideally the student is aligned with the runway, and at about 50 feet, begins a flare maneuver using the cyclic stick to slow the aircraft down. At 25 feet, the student is instructed to pull up smoothly on the collective stick in the left hand, which increases lift on all blades and creates an air cushion to "soften" the landing. The landing is basically the helicopter sliding down the runway. If you walk away, you pass.

Except on this day, I totally misjudged the runway and made the right turn way too early, and it resulted in me wasting half of the available runway. When I rolled out of my turn, my altitude was too high for the remaining runway, and I should have just rolled up the throttle power, made the call to the tower, and elected to do a "go around" and try again.

Nope, I decided under pressure that I was going to try to expedite the descent and squeeze the landing in. Bad call!

"I have the controls," he coolly said.

Game over! He remained extremely professional, made me do it again, and some other maneuvers, but we both knew I was toast.

When we landed back at the airfield, he simply told me that I did not meet the Army's standards and that I failed the P2 check ride. No drama. I acknowledged and performed my clean-up duties.

When I got back to the briefing room, Mr. Thorp just looked at me and shook his head in disappointment. He explained that we would do remedial training for the next few days, and then I would be tested again after all the other students. Just like that, I went from first to last.

And then he explained that if I "busted" the next P2 ride, I was going to be washed out. Cold hard truth...

Then I returned to the barracks where all of my friends were waiting to hear about my experience, only to have me walk in with a long face while breaking the news to them: I failed it. "What?!"

I wanted to crawl in a hole, and I worried that I was going to be the next dude to "wash out." I literally laid down on my bed and felt shame and embarrassment. I felt as though I let down my family, my fellow classmates, and of course Mr. Thorp.

Luckily, my buddies John Ramiccio, Bob Piselli, Kent Walker, Matt Weller, Paul Schlett and others kept things in perspective with barracks humor and conversation, but we all knew that I was in deep trouble.

I thought about the successful comeback I had from the knee injury, and it provided motivation. The next morning, we did our normal formation run, and by the time it was over, I was ready to make another go at it.

Thorp wasn't his witty and energetic self for a few days, as I assume he took some criticism from the other instructors on our performance.

Several days later, after finishing remedial training, I confidently retook and passed the P2 check ride. I decided that I was not going to go down without swinging.

Sometimes, you fail in a big, public way, and it is a hard pill to swallow. All you can do is accept that it happened, get up off the floor, hold your chin high, and drive on.

GET DIFFERENT PERSPECTIVES

With only one day remaining before the Phase 3 flight exam of Army pilot training, my best buddy John G. Ramiccio and I were in trouble. Neither one of us could consistently execute the critical maneuver needed to pass, the ILS (Instrument Landing System) approach.

The ILS approach allows a pilot to use cockpit instruments to safely land on an airport runway with minimal visibility. Regardless of the progress we had made so far in the first two phases, "washing out" of flight school was now a real possibility. Needless to say, we were stressed.

Ramiccio, nicknamed "Meech", was a natural pilot, and an all-around good man. Smart, focused and practical, he also had a fantastic sense of humor that usually lightened the mood when the stress level was high during flight school. To this day, I consider him a good friend even though we have only seen each other a few times in the last two decades.

Whereas the first two phases of flight school focused on basic maneuvers such as hovering and auto-rotation, the third phase included eight weeks of instrument training, including flight simulator work and actual flight time in the UH-1 Huey helicopter.

Instrument proficiency is necessary to manage Instrument Meteorological Conditions (IMC), weather conditions that require pilots to fly primarily by reference to instruments under instrument flight rules (IFR), rather than by outside visual references in Visual Meteorological Conditions (VMC).

We progressed from basic instrument procedures to flight on federal airways using FAA navigation systems and air traffic controlling agencies. If we could manage to successfully complete this phase, we would become instrument qualified and receive a helicopter instrument rating upon graduation.

The difficulty of learning how to fly the aircraft with instruments is that we had to demonstrate flight proficiency without actually looking outside of the aircraft. For flight school students who had just recently learned how to control the bird, this was quite a mental and physical challenge.

The experience was almost surreal, and could lead to dangerous illusions - Visual, Vestibular (related to fluid in the inner ear) or Proprioceptive (vibrations and feel) - that disorient the pilot and cause fatal mistakes, such as in the tragic crash of John F Kennedy, Jr.

Our Instrument Instructor Pilot was a small French fellow named Don Charest, on exchange from the French military. Instructor Charest was an intelligent, precise man who spoke in a high-pitched voice with a fast cadence.

During training, he made sure that we did not look outside of the aircraft (to cheat) by making us wear the "hood", a plastic helmet bill that funneled your vision into the cockpit. It was very unnerving at first, but learning to place confidence in the reliability of the instruments over your limited vision is the foundation of all competent instrument-rated pilots.

That day, I was in the right seat, sweating profusely as I struggled to fly the aircraft under the hood. Instructor Charest was in the left seat, with his metal teacher's pointer out, just lecturing away in his high-pitched voice.

Charest used the pointer to identify important information on the cockpit dials but had the highly annoying habit of tapping my helmet when he felt that I was not responding to his commands.

A good ILS approach keeps the horizontal and vertical lines pegged in a perfect cross; representing your accuracy in following the FAA's designated safe ILS approach into an airport.

However, if the vertical needle gets pegged all the way to the right of the instrument, you have strayed too far left, and need to correct by turning the aircraft right to re-intercept the course. If the horizontal needle is pegged to the bottom of the instrument, you are too high above the designated glide path and need to sharpen your descent to get back on the glide path.

As I focused my tunnel vision on the cockpit instruments, the vertical needle was pegged all the way to the right…it was a mess.

"Now turn back right, Frankie." Tap-tap-tap on the helmet.

I immediately followed his command and turned hard right but ended up overcorrecting, which then caused the needle to cross the center and peg to the far left. At that point, I could hear Charest barking out corrections.

"Come on. Turn left, Frankie." tap-tap-tap.

Somehow, even with his verbal guidance, I was unable to keep the aircraft on the ILS course into the airport. I could feel my blood starting to boil, as I literally was flying "S" patterns on my approach into the airport, totally unacceptable to the heartless flight examiner who I would have to face the next day.

Frustration was building between us, as he thought I was ignoring his advice, but it simply was not working. So, I blew a gasket and literally screamed at him in the middle of the approach. "I'm in a *&#@*%@ left turn!" He screamed back at me.

I actually thought that when we landed at the airport, there was going to be a fistfight. Fortunately, cooler heads prevailed moments later, or I would have been packing my bags the following morning.

Meech sat in the back "jump seat" just watching the ugliness, knowing that he was also not yet ready for the following day's exam.

On the way back to the barracks, Meech and I talked about the day's drama. We knew we were "dead-men walking." It was just a matter of time. We were going to "bust" the instrument flight exam in the morning, and the dream of earning the silver flight wings would likely end badly.

That night back at the barracks, just when we were out of solutions, I shared my dilemma with fellow student pilots, who had different instructors. From the discussion, they identified that the major problem was that we were overcorrecting in our turns in order to re-intercept the designated course, which was causing the overshoot and "S" turns.

Instead, they recommended that whenever we needed to get back on course, simply turn for a second or two then straighten the aircraft out and wait until the aircraft angle intercepted the course. It was a simple and practical solution, and we immediately understood how to implement it on the exam. The (mental) dark clouds parted, and the sun started to shine again!

The next morning, both Meech and I nailed the ILS approach during the flight exam. It was such a sweet turnaround in fortunes, in less than 24 hours, and paved the way to graduation day.

Whenever I think of that story, I am reminded of a valuable lesson:

Sometimes it helps to get another perspective.

Instructor Charest was certainly a skilled and knowledgeable instructor pilot. However, he could not seem to communicate to Meech and me the obvious solution on this one maneuver. Of course, he probably had already identified what was happening, but he did not effectively articulate in a manner that connected with us.

On the drive back from the flight line that day, I would have never imagined that a bunch of inexperienced fellow pilots would provide such a clear and workable solution. Sometimes, just when you are ready to accept defeat, you get lucky and stumble into a victory.

Whenever you are frustrated in life and run out of ideas, go get a fresh perspective from another source.

It just may work.

HELP OTHERS

Toward the completion of flight training, we were asked to submit our requests for duty stations. All of the soon-to-be aviators wanted to deploy to the Gulf for Operation Desert Storm, or a traditional posting like Fort Bragg, Fort Campbell, or maybe somewhere interesting like Germany.

Well, the Army did not really care for my preferences, and needed folks in Honduras Central America. So, four of us were headed for Soto Cano Airbase, Honduras, as part of the 4th Battalion, 228th Aviation Regiment.

When I first received my orders, I was a bit disappointed because we all wanted to go where the action was happening. Half of the Blackhawk class went to the Gulf, and the other half headed for Central America. I started to do a little research on our operations there and became intrigued by the possibilities of an interesting year.

I arrived in Honduras on a U.S. Air Force C-5 cargo plane with three of my fellow Blackhawk flight school classmates, 2LT Jeff Jepson, 2LT Bob Hammond and WO1 Paul Schlett. We started to feel right at home in the village of wooden "hootches," and it felt adventurous to be in one of the last "frontier" assignments.

Our unit of Army helicopters operated in the Central American countries such as Guatemala, Panama, El Salvador, Nicaragua, and Belize, and had numerous missions in support of our nation's foreign policy. We were involved in drug interdiction, Special Forces support, logistics, and the broad umbrella of missions called "Nation Building."

I especially enjoyed the Nation Building mission, because it allowed us to use our impressive military capabilities to help the poverty-stricken people of Honduras. The people were very appreciative and greeted us with warmth and hospitality. It felt good to be part of such a powerful organization using its might to improve the lives of the truly less fortunate.

One rewarding mission was the use of Blackhawk helicopters to reach remote villages, thousands of feet above sea level in rugged terrain, to deliver doctors and medical teams to administer immunizations, vaccinations, dental work and education on the devastation afflicted by diseases such as cholera and malaria.

The daily missions were grueling in that they often involved 8+ hours in the greenhouse-like cockpit, flying from one difficult landing zone to the next, in the scorching hot sun of Honduras. I was empowered to recognize how much my endurance had improved from the days of experiencing complete exhaustion after only one hour of training with Mr. Thorp.

As the aircraft approached the designated landing zones, we would look for the standard white flag placed by a community member to mark the best possible place to land the large bird. I usually experienced goose bumps on approach, as I spotted the long lines of people, who had probably walked for miles (in mountainous terrain), waiting to get rare healthcare.

It felt wonderful to be an American with the unique skills to help people.

As soon as the engines wound down and the rotor blades stopped turning, the village kids would dart toward the aircraft, surrounding us with admiration and enthusiasm before we could even open up the doors and climb down. It felt remarkable. The doctors immediately jumped out and purposefully began to do their fantastic work with the people.

We usually spent some time socializing with the kids, handing out goodies like writing/coloring tools and candy, and then the pilots usually left the crew chiefs to mind the aircraft while we strolled around the area and engaged in foreign diplomacy. The kids always followed us and talked, and it was an amazing experience!

In one village, a young girl wearing a yellow blouse and gray skirt, about 12 years old, seemed to engage us with an exceptional level of enthusiasm and relentlessness. She was very friendly, and it became clear that she was deaf and mute. Everywhere I walked, she followed me around with a positive attitude and a smile. I took a photo of her, and I think it made her day and mine!

The other community members were clearly aware of her limitations to communicate with me but seemed to embrace her uniqueness with understanding and assistance as the community tried (in broken English and Spanish) to communicate for her.

Although they must have known there were minimal resources available for her long-term support, the community expressed no resentment towards the girl in the yellow blouse. Instead, they expressed affection and camaraderie towards her.

It was an amazing juxtaposition of the powerful U.S. Army helping a village, only to witness the poverty stricken villagers helping one of their needy.

They were driven by the same fundamental purpose as us: to use our resources, skills, and talents in an effort that is larger than ourselves.

That sense of community, purpose, and acceptance of the little girl in the yellow blouse, in such a remote and poverty stricken area of the world, was reflected in the spirit of the U.S. soldiers.

To this day, I have not experienced a greater sense of fulfillment at work than the moments when my unique set of aviator skills, combined with the might of the greatest military on the planet, was employed to help the less fortunate.

In order to live a more meaningful life, make a difference in your community by finding a way to use your talents to help others who are less fortunate. It is more rewarding than money, power or prestige.

Prepare For The Worst

As mentioned in the previous chapters, my first duty assignment after flight school was with the 4th Squadron, 228th Aviation Regiment (Winged Warriors) in Honduras. Since the unit had the potential to be tasked with overwater missions based in Central America, squadron pilots needed to receive instruction in water survival.

Therefore, I was ordered to attend the water survival-training program at Naval Air Station ("NAS") Jacksonville (FL), along with my Blackhawk pilot buddies from flight school, Paul Schlett, Jeff Jepson and Bob Hammond.

As mission pilots in the Winged Warriors, we were required to learn the protocol and techniques used by aircrew members in the unlikely event that we crashed (and survived) at sea.

The expert in this area was the U.S. Navy. They had the knowledge, experience and facilities to properly train us on the precarious process of aircraft ditching, escaping and surviving at sea. The four of us hopped a cargo flight out of Soto Cano Airbase and headed for Jacksonville Florida for the Dunker/HEEDS (Helicopter Emergency Egress Device) training program.

The training was very intense, and highlighted the real difficulty in actually getting out of an aircraft if the dire situation ever occurred. I was a decent swimmer, but certainly no fan of deep, expansive water bodies.

However, the modified training for Army pilots was confined to the indoor training facility, because we were not expected to spend much time conducting over-water operations. In other words, this was training done to give our land loving crews a fighting chance if we ever ended up in the drink.

When I heard of our orders to attend, I was slightly surprised because most of the unit's missions occurred over the jungles, plains and mountains of Central America.

The first module of the training focused on knowledge of water survival techniques and use of equipment. A significant amount of the module was spent learning how to use the HEEDS, a small device that allows underwater breathing for short periods of time.

The HEEDS bottle fits nicely into the front of an aviator's flight vest, and the mouthpiece at the top is placed in the mouth to allow for 2-4 minutes of breathing at a depth of 20 feet.

Next we went through drown proofing, which is a method for surviving in water disaster scenarios without sinking or drowning. By floating in an upright attitude, with the face submerged and only lifting the mouth and nose above the surface when it is necessary to take a breath, it is possible to survive indefinitely, with minimal expenditure of energy.

To simulate real world conditions, all training was conducted in full flight gear, including flight suits, combat boots, gloves and helmets. They also taught us how to tie the uniform in a manner that allowed it to be used as a floatation device.

However, the highlight of the day was the work we did in the actual dunker, learning how to escape a downed aircraft. This phase included a "warm-up" dunk, and then executing four different sink-and-roll dunk scenarios.

As we sat strapped into to our seats, the dunker was slowly lifted above the pool by a small crane. The excitement running through my body was analogous to the feeling one gets at an amusement park as the slow, creaky roller coaster climbs to the apex before the first drop.

As I looked down, I saw several navy divers, dressed in bright yellow shirts, blue shorts, diving masks and black flippers. It was comforting to know the professional divers were there to rescue us in distress, but simultaneously unnerving to wonder why they needed so many of them in the water!

The first repetition was the easiest and referred to as the "warm-up." The dunker fell from about 10 feet into the pool, and Paul, Jeff, Bob and I felt the impact before the device began to sink. I placed one hand on the harness release and the other on a reference point of my window to aid in my escape.

The dunker sunk to about 5 feet deep in the water, but stayed in the upright impact position. We all followed the procedure, and exited our designated areas (our windows) in an orderly manner. The "warm-up" wasn't bad. One rep down!

After the "warm-up", there were four scenarios during the sink-and-roll portion of the training, each escalating the difficulty level.

In the first scenario, the "aircraft" hit and rolled, then we immediately unlatched our harnesses and escaped through the nearest exit. It was a little disorienting, but "good-to-go." We all surfaced, swam to the side of the pool in our soaking wet gear, and climbed out. We flashed a bunch of smiles, screamed "hoo-ahs!" and high-fives, and prepared for the next round. We've got this!

In the second scenario, we were informed that the escape would be through a single exit. This was a challenge for some of us, depending on the seat location. I was located farthest away from the designated exit, and would have to use a hand-over-hand method to escape. Additionally, the dunker instructors added an extra degree of difficulty and reality with time requirements.

The dunker slammed down onto the water, then sunk and rolled completely upside down, but we were instructed not to attempt to release the harnesses to escape during this period, which lasted about 10 long seconds. After the 10 seconds, we were upside down and disoriented, at which time we initiated our egress. I disconnected and made my way as planned to the identified exit by following my buddies, but I felt a bit of anxiety as the last to clear the "aircraft." I also managed to dodge a few combat boots from landing in my face. We all surfaced with a few "hoo-ahs!" but I think we all realized the game was changing.

In the third scenario, we were instructed to wear blacked-out goggles to simulate a night ditching without visibility, and we quickly recognized that this was getting more serious. After the crane lifted the dunker into place, there was a moment of complete silence that I am sure was enhanced by my lack of vision.

I could just visualize the heightened attention of the rescue divers as they looked up at this group of army dudes. All of us were relieved that they were in the water.

Then the dunker dropped without warning and slammed down onto the water. My body flinched and tightened up, and my hands squeezed the side of the window, the reference point the instructors taught us to use.

My inner ear fluid immediately sensed when the dunker experienced a rapid roll and sunk fast. As in scenario two, but with a bit more impatience, I waited until all motion had stopped, and then I disconnected, pulled toward the reference point, escaped through the exit nearest my seat, and quickly surfaced. Everyone made it to the surface, but I didn't hear any more bravado.

The fourth and final scenario presented a daunting challenge, and caused us the most concern. This was the scenario that would most resemble a real night ditching at sea, without the swells. This was the reason the U.S. Navy divers were hanging out in the pool.

All of us wore blacked-out goggles and would have to escape through the same exit. The instructors told us that this scenario could lead to panic because we were going to experience lack of vision while being disoriented and "trapped."

At this point, we were all very thankful that the Navy divers were underwater and ready to help immediately, if one of us were to experience distress.

Again, it was quiet before the drop, but this time I could feel and hear my heart pounding. I was in an absolute state of focus and alertness. You could feel the energy connecting us as if it was an electric wire.

Luckily, this time my seat positioning was relatively close to the exit. Unfortunately, my good buddy Paul Schlett had the worse position because he was furthest from the exit.

When the dunker hit the water, rolled, and sunk, I felt an immediate sense of urgency to get out. However, I followed the training, and waited the 10 seconds until the aircraft was upside down, then disconnected and walked hand-by-hand along the side until I felt a boot kick in my chest from either Bob or Jeff. I waited a few short seconds, and then continued until I got to the exit and managed to escape and surface. When I took off the goggles and climbed out of the pool, I noticed Jeff and Bob, but not Paul.

When I looked back into the pool, I could see commotion underwater with diver activity. Within a few seconds, the divers surfaced with Paul, who was clearly in distress. When they pulled him out of the pool, he leaned forward on his knees and puked.

Later, when we were reviewing what happened, Paul said that he got disoriented when his vest got caught on something in the dunker. The divers immediately recognized that he was in distress, and swam to him. In a real-life scenario, he would have been at the bottom of the dark sea.

However, this was only training, and although he swallowed a bit of water, he was fine. We all had a new story to tell over beverages!

We departed NAS Jax the following day and headed back to Soto Cano Airbase in Honduras. The training was excellent because it helped us to prepare for the worst-case scenario, although we certainly did not expect it to ever occur.

When you are prepared for the worst-case scenario, it empowers you and creates a coping mechanism to manage the contagious fear, panic and paralysis associated with things going horribly awry.

Your Life, Your Call

I was a 24-year-old helicopter pilot in the 4th Squadron, 228th Aviation Regiment ("Winged Warriors") based at Soto Cano Airbase, and I had recently qualified as "Pilot-In-Command" (PIC). Looking back now at the age of 52, it is quite remarkable how much responsibility the military placed in young adults. I was less than one year removed from completing flight training at Fort Rucker, Alabama and earning my silver aviator wings.

The key point here is that the military invests a lot of money and energy in training young people. The unit's mission was to provide air support to Joint Task Force Bravo in Central America, a collection of missions that included drug interdiction, nation building, and security operations.

This particular day, we were flying a two aircraft mission to enhance our knowledge of the amazing Honduran terrain, which included rugged mountain ranges, triple canopy jungles, beautiful beaches and vast swaths of barren land. This was truly an awesome playground for a young Blackhawk pilot, looking to sharpen his skills!

The plan was to depart Soto Cano, fly south toward the borders of El Salvador and Nicaragua to check out a few of our satellite outposts, then to fly north all the way up to the coast, stopping along the way to refuel when necessary at select points. We planned to be airborne for most of the day, making it an exhausting, yet valuable training exercise.

The Air Mission Commander (AMC) was a very experienced pilot named "Pete," in his forties. Pete was respected by all of the squadron's pilots as a calm, confident and skilled aviator. When he gave advice, people listened. Pete had a great sense of humor, was a fantastic storyteller, and just oozed the "devil-may-care attitude," straight out of central casting.

As a newly minted Pilot-In-Command, I was in charge of the second bird, and flying trail to Pete's Blackhawk. Each pilot had ultimate authority over his bird and aircrew, but the AMC had overall authority for the conduct of the mission.

Early on, the mission went smoothly as we flew south to orbit the top of Tiger Island Honduras, a U.S. communications post that sits in the Gulf of Fonseca and provides a clear view to the bordering countries of El Salvador and Nicaragua. After making a few approaches to practice our high altitude landings, we made our way back up from the south toward the rugged mountainous region in central Honduras.

At that point, the plan was to stop at an airport and refuel the birds with JP8 jet fuel, using Uncle Sam's credit card. As we approached the airport, Pete called me on the radio and asked, "Hey Frank, how is your bird doing on fuel?"

"We have sufficient fuel for the flight plan", I answered.

"Looks like clouds are building and bad weather may roll in, so we should consider skipping this fuel stop, and flying directly to the next fuel waypoint on the northern coast of Honduras", Pete suggested.

"Hold one, Pete." I responded, as my co-pilot and I did some quick calculations that concluded there was plenty of fuel to fly directly to the northern coastal town of Trujillo.

"Pete, we are ok to skip this fuel stop."

At that point, less than one year out of flight school at Fort Rucker, I didn't have enough experience to realize that this was the first in a series of bad judgments. Ultimately, this first mistake would lead to an anxiety filled problem that required luck to emerge in one piece. Pilot rule: Never pass gas. Always take fuel when available.

"Roger that", he confirmed. So we changed our course directly to Trujillo "as the crow flies", and climbed up to a couple of thousand feet. It was not long after when the weather surprisingly worsened with ominous dark clouds blocking our direct flight under VMC (Visual Meteorological Conditions).

"Hey Frank, let's deviate the course to the east to get around this weather, then we will get back on course on the other side of this storm front."

"Sure, no problem." I calmly responded as I banked the aircraft to the right to follow Pete's UH-60 Blackhawk.

Bad call number two. Pete's suggestion was not radical, as pilots often make creative weather decisions to accomplish the mission. However, it is never a good idea to try to outmaneuver Mother Nature. We should have turned around and went back to the airport and waited out the storm in the pilots' lounge.

The weather continued to worsen, and since we were in the rugged mountainous region of the country, and we had plenty of visibility above us, Pete suggested that we climb up above the weather to a high altitude to bypass the clouds and the mountains. I discussed it with my co-pilot, then with Pete's crew, and based on his confidence and experience, we agreed that it made sense.

"Yeah, I'm fine with that plan. Let's initiate a climb up to 10,000 feet, far above the tallest mountain in this region", I communicated. I was not yet worried, but I did get a sense that we were getting deeper into the mess and Mother Nature was not going to be easily outsmarted.

Note: Flying in a third world country like Honduras is different than a country like the USA with advanced air traffic control and radar approach capabilities. In the USA, we would have called the regional air traffic controller authority, reported the situation and asked for radar vectors for safe passage to the airport, and we would have utilized IFR (Instrument Flight Rules) to ensure safe and effective navigation. Honduras in 1991 did not have very good air traffic capabilities outside of the cities like Tegucigalpa and San Pedro Sulu. It was mostly uncontrolled airspace.

So, we climbed up above the clouds without incident and proceeded directly to the designated landing airport. The plan was to descend once we got closer to the destination. At that point, with all of the flight deviations, and the higher burn rates involved in the climbs, our fuel levels started to get low. I made a call to Pete.

"Pete, we are getting kind of low on fuel and need to initiate our descent".

Pete agreed and confirmed that he was getting low on fuel also, as the birds were now above the clouds at 10,000 feet. The problem was that because of the poor weather services in the country, and the lack of air traffic control, we had to wait until we found a break in the cloud deck before we could descend in a region with mountains. We flew a little longer, and my co-pilot had our location estimated on a map, although it would have been nice to have current technology for accuracy.

Then, the low fuel light came on, to indicate 20 minutes remaining, but of course, that was just an estimate. Could be more, and could be less. My stress level went up because a Blackhawk without fuel has all the aerodynamic characteristics of a rock.

That was when Pete saw an opening in the cloud cover and abruptly dove his aircraft down through it. This was crazy since we were not sure the location of the mountains. One minute he was there, and then he was gone. By the time my bird made it to that opening, it did not look too promising and we continued north beyond it.

Again, we were still at the high altitude of 10,000 feet, and over mountains that we could not see due to the cloud cover. Pete could not help us now. I chatted with the co-pilot, and we decided that the best course of action was to remain at high altitude until we estimated that we were covering the coastline, then we would initiate a blind descent through the clouds until we broke out of the bottom.

With the fuel light flashing, and without radar vectors for guidance, we began our descent into the clouds. Not long after we initiated the decent, the crew chiefs saw a hole in the clouds and we broke out.

When we landed at the local airport and taxied in, I was fuming and could not wait to give Pete a piece of my mind. We shut the aircraft down, and I stormed over to confront him, only to find him chomping on a big cigar, with his feet up and a big smile on his face.

Pete said "whoa, we dodged a bullet there! I'm sorry for how it played out Frank, but I thought that you were going to follow me down through the opening in the clouds." He acknowledged the mistakes in his judgment, but it was clear that he had a strong belief in his ability to pull a Houdini and get out of trouble. After so many years in Army Aviation, he had developed that attitude.

After I dropped a few profanity-laced sentences in a spirited rant, he stood up, smiled and gave me a big hug while laughing. Then he said, "Your Life, Your

Call". Poetic. It was always hard to stay mad at Pete for very long...

There were many mistakes that could have gotten us killed that day, including "passing gas", challenging bad weather, and climbing above the clouds without instrument flight capability. However, the life lesson I learned that day was that sometimes the experts could be wrong.

It is critical to seek advice from the best in your field, but never outsource the final decision to anyone who doesn't bear a similar risk as you.

Listen to the best counsel on the subject, think deeply about the pros and cons, and then make your call. It's your life.

As we headed back to Soto Cano Airbase, I recognized that I no longer was a student pilot under the protective wing of Mr. Dennis Thorp.

I had to think like a Pilot-In-Command.

ACCEPT CRITICISM

In 1992, after finishing a year flying difficult missions in Central America, I transferred to the 4th Squadron, 11th Armored Cavalry Regiment in Germany. This was the vaunted unit that defended the infamous Fulda Gap on the old Cold War border.

For decades, the "Blackhorse" regiment patrolled the Fulda Gap, which was dubbed "the forward edge of freedom." The unit was big, formal, and filled with bravado and very experienced and capable senior aviators. The unit was famous for operating at a high level of readiness and precise standards.

As a new pilot in the squadron, I was laser-focused on proving my competence to the seasoned aviators. After demonstrating my proficiency in the first year and passing all of the training requirements, I once again earned the Pilot-In-Command "PIC" designation.

This meant that I could be in-charge of an aircrew and would be responsible for the overall performance, safety, and welfare of the crew and aircraft. In retrospect, that was quite a level of responsibility to give a 25-year-old, but consistent with the overall military.

It felt good to get the designation because I had been operating in this capacity in the untamed airspace of Central America, flying "real world" missions into areas that were tactically challenging and potentially hostile to U.S Forces. Because this experience was so early into my career, only one year after graduating from flight training, I had an over-inflated view of my significance, capabilities, and wisdom.

The Air Squadron's Stetson Troop had flown multiple helicopters to Berlin to conduct a tactical field exercise, and I was one of the PICs involved. The exercise ended after a few days of training, but when it was time for my aircraft to depart, I decided that the weather was too precarious for the flight back to our home airfield.

So, I made the command decision to delay and told my crew to shut the aircraft down and go back to the hangar where the remaining crews were situated. After tying down the bird, we walked into the office.

Immediately, I was questioned by a well-respected senior pilot named Jim Garst in his booming voice, in front of the rest of the pilots in a way I perceived as condescending. He demanded to know why I had not executed the plan and gone back to Sickles Army Airfield in Fulda.

Jim's very direct approach caught me off guard, and it embarrassed my fragile ego that he publicly doubted my decision. After all, had I not demonstrated to him my talents and judgment before the Instructor Pilots approved me as PIC?

He then implied that I had not actually checked the weather, a very simple task required, and I quickly took it personally and lost my composure.

Well, somehow this simple disagreement about the appropriateness of the weather turned heated and almost physical. To me, it was not about the weather decision but it was about the respect that I craved from senior aviators like Jim Garst.

Before long, we were nose-to-nose, ready to scrap, when another pilot named Kevin Callaway, a 6'6" former football player, separated us. Tensions were high, and at that moment I actually believed that I was correct.

Later on, when I cooled down and talked to other highly respected pilots like CW2 Mike Richardson, I was surprised that most of them perceived my actions as overly sensitive, insubordinate, wrong and unacceptable. I felt like a complete idiot.

Several aviators told me that the old bull Jim Garst was well within his mandate as a senior instructor pilot to question a new pilot to the unit. After all, this was the way that the squadron set and regulated its own high standards: a system of very direct and candid feedback.

I gathered the aircrew together, with my tail between my legs, and flew back home. In a day's time, after the episode had been replayed in my mind a hundred times, I realized my explosive reaction was based on my insecurity as the new pilot in the unit.

I approached him outside the hangar, apologized, and told him that my father always taught me to admit when I was wrong. He just stared expressionlessly at me for what seemed like a minute of silence, cigarette hanging out of the corner of his mouth. Then, I will never forget what Jim Garst said next.

"Frank, I appreciate your integrity and willingness to acknowledge your overreaction. Your stock has just doubled in my mind."

I was so relieved that he handled it with so much class and dignity, and that he saw no need to rub my nose in the regret.

The story got even better, because a couple of years later in my career, I arrived at a new unit. Can you guess who was serving as the Chief Instructor Pilot?

That's right, the old bull, Jim Garst! However, now I had a powerful sponsor, and it was a good development for my career.

Sometimes, tensions can run high in the workplace, and people can cross over the threshold into taking it personally and becoming angry. Certainly, there are times when you have to stand your ground, but you must understand if the reason for the anger and defensiveness is associated with the current subject in disagreement, or just simple insecurity with constructive criticism.

Growth comes from making improvements, and that cannot happen unless you have clear awareness. Constructive criticism is a gift to anyone interested in self-improvement and achieving ambitious goals because it highlights areas of weakness that you can immediately improve upon.

The next time you are directly criticized and it angers or hurts you, pause a few minutes before responding to consider the reason behind your disabling emotions.

Are you upset because the person said it, or are you upset because it is true?

STAY CALM

In the beautiful countryside of Fulda Germany, the U.S. Army's Thunder Horse helicopter squadron was about to launch a night training exercise using multiple aircraft flying at high speeds and low altitudes. The squadron was the air component of the famed tank-heavy 11th Armored Cavalry Regiment, the first line of defense during the Cold War.

Although a few years had passed since the fall of the Berlin Wall and the collapse of the Soviet Union, the 11th ACR was still in place along the "forward edge of freedom" in the event that the Russians changed their minds.

The unit still participated in military pageantry complete with cavalry officers riding black stallions to the sounds of a marching band, and troopers wearing the Stetson hats, riding boots with spurs, swords, and scarves. We simply traded in the old western Cavalry horses for modern helicopters and tanks.

Camaraderie was high in the unit, and I had many fantastic friends like Theo Bell, Vince Arnold, Kelvin Martinez, Cliff Mead, Pat Williams, Dan Christ, Jim Nelson, Kevin Callaway, Larry Williams, Mark

McGhee, John Helms, Rod Sookoo, Mark Mata, Chris Sebastian and many more. Additionally, my old flight school buddy Kent Walker had been assigned to the squadron's Apache Troop, so we reconnected and became roommates in a downtown apartment.

Air Cav pilots had to earn their spurs by demonstrating physical fitness, aviator competence, soldier skills like marksmanship and land navigation, and a highly motivated attitude. The process to earn the spurs was rigorous, challenging and rewarding.

One task necessary for a pilot to earn his (In 1992, it was an all-male unit of 2,000+) spurs was to demonstrate the ability to navigate the aircraft along sensitive Cold War borders at night.

Although I had already earned my spurs, the purpose of this particular training flight was to sharpen our navigation skills at night. We used night vision goggles (NVGs) to see without lights, which provided a significant tactical advantage. Looking through NVGs is similar to looking through two toilet paper rolls, with everything tinted in green.

Our Air Mission Commander was an excellent leader named Captain Hastings, who was flying in an aircraft toward the end of our group.

He had delegated the navigation of the flight of Blackhawks to the pilots in the lead aircraft, who happened to be another guy named Patrick and me.

The Squadron Commander, a tough and demanding old-school U.S. Cavalry Colonel, was flying above us to observe our proficiency. The Colonel, in an attempt to simulate real world urgency, pressured us to launch before we were actually ready to fly into the darkness of the night.

Patrick and I made the mistake of rushing under pressure, as we were not completely ready with the map and navigation systems, and that small error began to snowball shortly.

I informed the flight of Blackhawks that we were ready to depart, by radioing the standard warning to all aircraft over the internal net.

"Pitch pull in five, four, three, two, one…"

The aircraft departed into the dark countryside over the plains of Fulda. Not long after departing and making a few turns, we noticed that our navigation system was not set up properly, so we navigated the old fashioned way with a map and flashlight, as the Blackhawks skimmed along the terrain of the dark countryside.

At some point in the flight, we got really disoriented. Under NVGs, it is easy to mistake terrain features.

That was when the hollering started over the radios, and it was downright ugly.

The Colonel, testing our ability to manage chaos, was screaming at Captain Hastings by using every combination of words that were imaginable about how bad this training exercise was going. He wanted to know why Hastings was unable to demonstrate better command and control over his formation.

It was painful to hear, and I know that Hastings felt embarrassed and humiliated about the public chewing-out, even though it was not his fault that we were lost.

It was ours.

This radio exchange was surreal to hear, with the Colonel hammering him to get this problem corrected ASAP, and Hastings then talking to us as if nothing was wrong.

It was like we were relaxing on the beach, drinking smoothies. Star Trek's Spock had nothing on this guy Hastings. The Captain was cool under pressure. He never passed the venom down to us, which would have been understandable. He simply took the pain and worked to solve the problem.

Do you know what he said to us in between the Colonel's tirades?

Not much, because he knew we were good pilots simply in a bad situation. He calmly helped us figure out our position, and guided us back on course.

It was a moment of leadership that I will always remember.

Every pilot on that training mission gained an immense amount of respect for Captain Hasting's leadership under pressure, and his decision to filter out the harsh noise and work calmly. It was the talk of the unit for days.

After all, this occurred as several helicopters were slicing through the night by skimming the treetops at more than 120 mph, in the dark...

What did I learn from this episode that I try to remember?

Stay Calm, and Don't Criticize in Public.

Public criticism rarely produces a better outcome, because it adds unnecessary negativity to an already bad situation. Public criticism puts people on the defensive, demoralizes them, and creates resentment. This usually leads to lower productivity and inhibits forward thinking.

Think about a time when someone has publicly criticized you. What did you think about over the next 24 hours of your life? I bet your thoughts were focused on every conceivable reason why you were in the right, or not really at fault.

Rarely does it motivate the person to make the changes necessary to correct the problem. Even if the criticism is accurate, it forces them to rationalize, justify and explain the behavior. It is human nature to protect our pride when under attack, rather than to admit fault.

Think about a time when you screamed at, or criticized, a person in front of others. How did it turn out? Were they appreciative of your perceived "constructive criticism" that probably came across as a public rebuke? Did they enthusiastically accept your "advice"?

Remember, some people carry the resentment of public humiliation with them their entire lives. It hurts.

Humans search for approval, but we dread condemnation.

The next time a family member, co-worker or friend is in distress, and their mistake is exposed for the world to see, avoid the impulse to criticize, and instead calmly, privately and positively help them to solve the problem.

You will avoid creating an enemy, and immediately earn the respect of all who witness your actions.

OWN YOUR FAILURE

In 1994, when I lived on the Mediterranean Sea island of Cyprus, I made a very serious mistake that could have been fatal...

At the time, I was a pilot in the U.S. Army, living on a Royal British Air Force base as part of a small contingent of American aircrews.

Our task was to fly the Beirut Air Bridge, a mission using UH-60 Blackhawk helicopters to provide support to the U.S Embassy in Beirut. The Air Bridge provided the only safe mode of transportation for U.S diplomats and security personnel between Cyprus, a stable island nation, and the U.S Embassy in the war-torn city of Beirut, Lebanon.

The mission originated in the aftermath of the 1983 Marine Barracks bombing that infamously took the lives of several hundred marines and government personnel.

The BAB mission was flown in the night at very low levels (100 - 500ft) to reduce the exposure to radar detection and hostile action. It required the skilled use of night vision goggles, dubbed "NVGs", and a totally "blacked-out" light configuration on the helicopters. Flying with NVGs is similar to looking through two toilet paper rolls with everything in a greenish color.

The tricky and most dangerous part of the mission was the transition from flying from the dark sea, into a brightly illuminated city, and vice versa on the way back out of Beirut. It was complicated because the pilots had to switch from using the NVGs (aided vision) to looking under them with "unaided" vision, into the bright lights of the city. It could be very disorienting, and we often had to reference cockpit instruments to get our bearings.

I had flown the mission numerous times and felt confident executing it. I had volunteered to remain in Cyprus longer than the standard rotation, because I liked living on the beautiful island and the adventure. I was perhaps the most experienced BAB mission aviator in the unit.

The result was that I was often tasked with conducting the pre-flight briefing to all aircrew members and passengers. I always stressed the danger to the pilots and aircrew members of the transition from aided to unaided flight on the coastline of Lebanon, especially on a zero illumination night (no starlight).

One dark night, after spending less than two minutes on the embassy-landing zone, I led two helicopters back out of the brightly lit city, toward the dark sea. I was the Pilot-in-Command, and there were a co-pilot, door gunner and crew chief in our aircraft.

Behind our "bird" was another Blackhawk following us. Adding to the normal difficulty of the transition from light to darkness was the steep descent that the helicopters had to take to get back down from the embassy, at a higher elevation, to the coastline.

Additionally, the radios were very active with necessary communications between our aircraft and other U.S. assets in the area. Finally, there was the added distraction of the ole' APR-39, a radar warning device in the cockpit to detect and audio warn us about any hostile weapons system "painting" the helicopters with radar as we flew by non-friendly areas. A lot was going on.

Anyway, flying at 150 knots (~mph), less than 100 feet above the ground and in a very steep descent to follow the contour down to the coastline, my co-pilot and I became distracted for a second as we crossed over the beach as we headed back into the "abyss" of a very dark night. The unaided eye could distinguish very little difference between the water and horizon.

At that point, when I should have switched back to using NVGs, checked the instruments, and leveled off the aircraft at 100 feet, I unknowingly continued the descent and we were headed right into the dark sea!

Luckily, crew chief PFC Pennington, only 19 years old, was looking into the cockpit at the radar altimeter and yelled... "Watch the @$#!%* altitude, Sir!"

I was on the controls and looked down at the radar altimeter and it read a mere 33 feet. Yikes! 33 Feet!

I applied full power with the collective control in my left hand, deep left pedal for anti-torque, and yanked back on the cyclic stick with my right hand to arrest the descent... and waited...and somehow we didn't hit the water!

I climbed back up to 100 feet and set a course for a home in the complete darkness. For over 100 miles, in complete darkness, no one said a single word.

The hour flight back to Cyprus was difficult for me to stay focused on the mission, and not beat myself up over a mistake that almost cost four lives. I was numb with regret, disappointment, and anger (at myself). My mind wandered to what my crew must be thinking about me right now. And I was surprised that I made such a mistake, after being so clear in my pre-flight warning to everybody else on the dangers of that very transition. Ugggh.

We were also very lucky that night in another way, in that we didn't have a second event. The mental state that I was stuck in was not conducive to diagnose and quickly handle such problems.

When we landed, I pulled the crew aside and apologized for the mistake. I felt very down that night because I knew that if the young soldier would not have spoken up when he did, CNN would be running a story of a "Blackhawk Down off the coast of Beirut". Everyone would have assumed hostile action, and not the truth: pilot error.

What did I learn from that harrowing night?

The best way to handle a mistake is to verbally acknowledge personal fault.

It is natural to make excuses…share blame with the co-pilot for not catching the error, or point out all the things that distracted me.

However, the bottom line was that I messed up big, and it was a burden removed from my shoulders when I publicly admitted it to the aircrew. I believe they appreciated the accountability.

It is always better to encourage subordinates to feel empowered and able to speak up and identify something that is abnormal.

Besides Pennington speaking up, the second most important factor that saved us was the open communication environment of the crew.

I give myself credit for this because as part of my pre-flight briefing, I always asked all aircrew members to speak up if they saw something wrong, regardless of their rank or position.

When you make a mistake, it is best not to dwell and mope around.

Moping around usually results in a second mistake. Just accept it, commit to learning from it, and move on. Own it!

When time allows, always review what happened and formulate lessons learned, and a procedure to reduce the chances that you make the same mistake again.

When you handle a mistake correctly by taking responsibility and acknowledging your human faults, the painful experience eventually makes you a better person.

FACE YOUR FEARS

I thought my biggest fear had finally caught up with me: I was going to be stranded at sea, in the middle of the night.

It was 1994, and I was the pilot-in-command of a U.S. Army Blackhawk helicopter, one of two birds flying over the Mediterranean Sea headed from the island of Cyprus to Beirut, Lebanon. About fifty miles from land, in the middle of the night, I got a radio call from the second aircraft.

"Eagle 32, you have smoke billowing out of your number 1 engine."

Throughout my life, I had a fear of crossing any large body of water via bridges, boats or planes. The thought of struggling to survive in a massive body of water, especially night, was a secret fear.

Like most people, I simply tried to avoid situations associated with this fear and went on with my life. I certainly didn't expect the fear to alter the trajectory of my life path. I went to the beach, jumped in the water, and even rode jet skis and such...but always stayed within swimming distance of the coastline.

Instead of the Navy, I joined the Army, expecting to avoid flying over large bodies of water...just jungles, woods, and deserts.

You know where this story is going, right?

Then, in an unexpected turn of events, I was assigned to one of the *few* U.S. Army units that actually specialized in over-water, night flying missions. What the heck!

Aviators in the Eagle Flight Detachment gained proficiency in U.S. Navy ship landing and sea rescue operations. Additionally, we received excellent training at the U.S. Navy's Water Survival Training Center at Naval Air Station Jacksonville (Florida). During missions, we wore specialized "Mustang Suits" to improve survivability in cold water if stranded at sea.

Back to the story...

After receiving the alarming radio call from the other aircrew, I was concerned that where there was smoke, there was (likely) fire. Having a fire onboard an aircraft in flight, at night, over miles of water, was a very sobering thought, and would present quite a challenge.

My co-pilot and I began an analysis of the cockpit instruments to verify indications of a fire, including engine oil temperature, pressure, etc. Everything looked normal.

I began to put the aircraft in slow "S" turns to get a better visual on our problem, and I asked my crew chief in the back to look out and identify the "smoke."

"Yes sir, we have smoke coming out the left side."

I was perplexed. More than one person had confirmed "smoke", but everything inside the cockpit and the aircraft performance was normal. We continued to try to solve the mystery, but without the ability to simply land and evacuate the aircraft, and no real fire fighting capabilities onboard, the options were limited.

I began to think about the steps necessary to prepare the crew for the dreaded "ditching at sea," in the dark. Although I had deliberately tried to avoid ever being in this fearful situation, it looked like I was in it.

Interestingly at that moment, because of training, preparation and knowledge, I was not scared, but focused. Good training.

I had practiced this maneuver in the flight simulator after learning the process at NAS Jax. The procedure would begin with the pilot-in-command bringing the aircraft to a hover over the dark sea using night vision goggles with no reference points. At that point, the crew chief would kick the inflatable raft out the door into the sea, and then the rest of the crew would jump into the darkness of water and deploy their "water wings" (think inflatable arm bands). They would swim to, and board, the raft until the other aircraft was clear to commence rescue operations.

Next, I (the lonely pilot-in-command) would have the responsibility of flying the bird away from the crew a "safe distance", and then the real fun would begin. It required the unnerving procedure of ditching, waiting than exiting a submerged and dark aircraft as it was singing to the bottom of the Mediterranean Sea.

It involved a controlled crash, engine shutdown, violent moment of blades impacting the water, then waiting until the aircraft had rolled upside down into the complete darkness of the Mediterranean Sea. If you tried to evacuate before the blades stopped, you risked being killed by the moving blades.

At that point, I would use my training from the DUNKER/HEEDS training at NAS Jax, and unhook my seat harness, exit the dark aircraft and swim to the surface. I knew how hard that would be to accomplish.

If I were lucky enough to surface before being trapped in the sinking helicopter headed to the bottom of the sea, I would orient myself to the crew in the inflatable raft by finding their strobe lights, and start the long swim in high seas to their position.

Easy, right?

But, luckily, we were not at that point of ditching just yet, because there was no actual fire, just "smoke". So, we continued to analyze the problem while keeping the other helicopter crew updated.

Just as I was starting to feel like a refreshing night dip in the sea was inevitable, a light bulb came on inside my head.

I wondered if our auxiliary fuel tanks might be the problem. The "Aux" tanks were configured as attachments to allow for longer flight range by transferring extra fuel into the main tanks. Each Aux tank had a "shut-off valve" that automatically stopped pumping fuel into the main tanks when they were full.

If that valve were malfunctioning, the aux tank would continue to try to transfer fuel into a full main tank. The resulting mist, caused by the spewing of fuel out the side of the aircraft, may just look like "smoke" to aviators looking through night vision goggles. I reached down, and flipped down the aux fuel transfer switch, and made a call to the other aircraft.

"Eagle 15, this is Eagle 32...is the "smoke" still coming out?"

"Negative, it's stopped."

My crew chief stuck his head out the window and confirmed.

"No "smoke," sir."

Good gracious. Everything was fine, but I felt like I had finally faced my fear, and outmaneuvered it with my mind.

With energy and focus, we avoid fearful situations and attempt to cast them aside. However, even though it takes a long and circuitous path, the boomerang of our fears eventually comes right back.

Do you have a fear of public speaking before large crowds, trusting others, or a crawling critter?

Everyone has a fear.

Some people just hide it well and spend their lives taking actions to keep out of situations that may bring them face to face with the fear. Ultimately, the Boomerang of Fear comes back to you.

Instead of running from it, begin by verbally acknowledging your fear, as this is the first step in dealing with it. Next, write down the details of how and why you have this fear, which will "externalize" the fear.

Third, spend some time on the Internet learning about the fear.

Finally, recognize the actual probabilities of it happening. In the worst-case, outcomes are likely low.

At the end of the day, knowledge and confrontation mitigate fear.

Read For Knowledge

As mentioned in earlier chapters, I was part of the Eagle Flight Detachment based on the beautiful Mediterranean Island of Cyprus and supported the U.S. State Department with the Beirut Air Bridge.

The three-month rotation was a fantastic experience. Since I didn't have many obligations in Germany, I volunteered to extend a total of 11 months in 1994. We lived in modest accommodations at Royal Air Force Base Akrotiri and I developed many life-long friendships with so many good people like John Bentley, Aaron Nelson, Rachel Stuart, Gary Jorgensen, Nichola Deans, Patrick McDonald, Scott Keeney, Michael Huggins and many more.

We were provided with two Mazda 626 sedans and a van for our daily transportation needs. Fortunately, the commander allowed us to use the vehicles for off-duty activities, which often included exploring the island's beautiful destinations.

I liked that the flight mission was challenging, adventurous and dangerous; a nice match for young

American pilots hoping to make a contribution to the nation.

The added benefit of the temporary assignment to the detachment was the fantastic lifestyle on the island. We were a small unit of soldiers, so the culture was significantly more relaxed and autonomous than in a traditional Army unit.

To maintain a low profile, consistent with diplomatic work, uniforms were only required on flight missions and the grooming standards were eased a bit to blend in with the local population. It was not uncommon for us to walk around in beach clothes and flip-flops until it got dark and the mission pre-flight process started.

Since night missions required the appropriate crew rest, we did not have to participate in the normal U.S. Army physical training at the crack of dawn. We were free to exercise on our own, which provided an amazing opportunity to cross-train using beach runs, cycling, the RAF gym, and other interesting activities. We were self-motivated soldiers, so the commander never had a problem with any of us maintaining fitness standards.

Our living facility included a decent kitchen for those who preferred to prepare their own meals, or we could eat at the RAF Officer or Enlisted clubs, local restaurants or order take-out.

We were the proverbial night owls: We worked at night, slept in the mornings, and socialized and exercised in the late afternoon. On the nights that we did not have a flight mission, we were free to take in the local nightlife, and our fun-loving group of young aviators never passed on those opportunities.

The extraordinary range of Cyprus' beauty spans from the clear blue water at the white-sandy beaches, along the rugged cliff coasts, to the nearby Troodos Mountains, a scenic range that surprisingly hosts four (snow) ski resorts. The climate was warm, sunny, and consistent throughout the year.

The Cypriot people, of Greek descent on the southern part of the island (since the 1974 Civil War), were incredibly friendly, gracious and willing to share their culture.

We made many friends with the locals, especially our friends Jimmy and Nana who owned a fantastic Mexican restaurant and a popular nightclub. They were absolutely gracious hosts and never allowed their American friends to pay in their establishments.

When we utilized our diplomatic privileges and drove across the border into the Northern Republic of Cyprus, the beaches, casinos, and people (of Turkish descent) were equally as beautiful and welcoming.

The island is a tourist destination and "gateway" between Europe and the Middle East, therefore the lifestyle on this tiny island is unique because of the opportunity to socialize with people from the Middle East, Africa, Eastern, and Western Europe and the Scandinavian countries. It was a true melting pot of different people, arriving in a festive mood with the intent to enjoy their time in this Mediterranean paradise.

One evening, I was at a social event in the coastal city of Limassol, and I struck up an interesting conversation with a beautiful woman from the Middle East. She was thoughtful, intelligent and well educated, and told me she lived in London but was just visiting the island of Cyprus. I asked where she was from, and she gave a short but complicated answer.

"Palestine."

Hmmm. As the conversation continued, my mind raced to fix "Palestine" on the maps that I had studied and used during our numerous flight missions.

"I know the Middle East, and Palestine is not on the maps!" I thought to myself as I held a smile.

My brain recalled some superficial knowledge of the Palestinian Liberation Organization "PLO," and the biblical reference to Palestine, but nothing concrete to advance this conversation without exposing my ignorance of her culture and history. I felt a bit embarrassed, although I am not sure that she realized it because the conversation continued on.

Public search engines like Google, easily accessed on today's smart phones, were not available at the time. If so, I would have excused myself to the bathroom in the middle of the conversation and quickly studied-up!

The next day, I went over to the airbase library to learn about Palestine. The librarian directed me to the classic book by the New York Times journalist Tom Friedman, titled "From Beirut To Jerusalem," and I consumed it in a matter of days.

I was absolutely intrigued with the history of the region and its belligerent parties. I had been operating in the area without a true understanding of the age-old conflict. The history was so vast, complex and ancient that I decided to read another book on the subject... then another.

I tried to read contrarian perspectives on the same history. With a subject as contentious as Middle Eastern history, there was an abundance of informed, yet vastly different viewpoints. With an understanding of the region's historical context as a foundation, I learned quite a bit about her background and geopolitical views embedded in her short answer of "Palestine".

Up until that point in my life, age 28, I read mandatory materials such as school assignments and military training manuals, and could effortlessly recite the knowledge. For the consumption of news, entertainment, and self-development, I read newspapers, sports magazines, and autobiographies of successful people.

However, most of my reading was for the purpose of learning the common rules and attributes of successful people, and not to gain different perspectives on complex issues. Of course, studying the stories and lessons of successful people are extremely important in the pursuit of personal achievement and team building, but not the basis for understanding the larger world, and how history may shape the future.

So, "I learned how to read" for nuance, perspective, and historical depth, at the age of 28.

I started sharing the history with my fellow soldiers, and before I knew it, our commanding officer asked me to develop an educational briefing so incoming aircrew would have a historical understanding of the region's conflicts. The briefing audience expanded over time to include all visiting personnel and dignitaries. Before I knew it, it was a full-fledged "dog and pony" show.

I was labeled "the Middle Eastern expert" by my fellow soldiers, and was even (falsely) rumored to have attended Harvard's JFK School of Government!

I learned some valuable lessons from this episode...

We experience pivotal moments in life when the intrigue (or embarrassment) of a human interaction prompts us to follow-up intellectually. However, at this fork in the road, few people actually follow through, even though it often leads to new opportunities for personal growth.

When you have these chance encounters with interesting people who trigger intellectual curiosity, go with your intuition and see where it takes you.

Studying history from various perspectives highlights the nuance and complexity of human life, and will teach you how to "walk a mile in another person's shoes." It is very convenient and digestible for us to boil down complex issues to a simple slogan, but effective leaders need to understand the larger perspective and historical context.

If we want to create a better future society, with a greater understanding of humanity, we need to teach children to look at issues from different vantage points, instead of the simple 'good versus bad' story format.

History is often taught to children in an "elementary" manner so that the outcome is favorable to the victor. The assumption is made that children will not be comfortable, or able to grasp the complexity. I remember how clearly defined the line was drawn between good and evil throughout my childhood education in history.

"The Cowboys are the good guys, and the Native Americans are the bad guys, right?"

In reality it is complicated, and it depends on your perspective, based on one's knowledge of human history. Instead of simple slogans, let's teach kids how to think using multiple perspectives, and they will grow up to be more effective and thoughtful citizens.

Hopefully, they will learn how to read a bit earlier in life. After all, it took me until the ripe old age of twenty-eight before I learned how to read.

Dedicate To A Cause

I believe that our sense of purpose is strongest when dedicated to a cause larger than personal interests. I experienced this first hand in 1995 while serving as a pilot in the 498th MEDEVAC Company at Fort Benning, Georgia.

The unit's primary mission was to conduct air ambulance operations in support of Fort Benning, including Ranger and Airborne training. Often times we transported broken Airborne soldiers off the jump zone when parachute accidents occurred, or flew injured candidates from the grueling Army Ranger training facilities in the Darby, swamp or mountain phases.

Additionally, the unit was tasked with providing AERO MEDEVAC support to the poor rural communities in the Southeast who did not have the funding to support helicopter based rescue operations. This mission gave us tremendous fulfillment, as we helped our fellow citizens by using our unique skills and powerful assets.

We landed on rural roads that were shut down by State Troopers, and whisked away critically injured citizens to the emergency room to preserve lives after car accidents.

The third mission that we performed was the highly fragile mission of neonatal transport of premature babies who were housed in incubators. I never tried so hard in my career to touch down so softly.

The unit was filled with patriotic aircrew members, who took pride in their work. Aviators like John Vance and Moses McIntosh, and fantastic Combat Medics like David Kimball.

On May 17th, 1995, CW2 James Gardner and I were pilots on alert duty with SSG James R. Hernandez (medic), SGT Tedman Graves (medic) and SP4 Clinton Reilman (crew chief). Unexpectedly, we received a tasking for an emergency mission to fly from Fort Benning to Atlanta to rescue a critically ill retired soldier named Russell Gilbert.

Similar to well rehearsed firefighters, we ran out to the bird, and each of us performed our pre-arranged tasks and had the bird airborne in a few minutes. Teamwork was key.

When we arrived to pick up Mr. Gilbert, Captain Daniel J. Prescott, the head nurse, informed us that Mr. Gilbert was in bad shape, as his oxygen saturation was critical and Prescott was running out of oxygen. We got airborne quickly and headed to Peachtree Dekalb airport, where a VA ground ambulance was supposed to meet us to complete the transfer.

However, when we descended rapidly into the LZ (Landing Zone), we noticed the ground transportation was not there. At that point, Captain Prescott told Jim and I that this was a critical situation and we could not wait around for ground transportation. We decided to fly him directly to the VA hospital even though we did not have preflight clearance or a known LZ.

As we launched back into the sky, Prescott told us that the oxygen had run out, and Mr. Gilbert's situation had degraded to life threatening. We pushed the Blackhawk to maximum speed, and arrived at the VA hospital in the quickest time possible.

Jim and I took the liberty of aggressively landing in a nearby field, which surprised some hospital employees who probably thought an invasion was underway. Hernandez flagged down a ground ambulance, and Mr. Gilbert was rushed into emergency. He survived, and it was due to the actions of the entire crew and excellent leadership by Captain Prescott.

If the day had ended on that note, it would have been one of my favorite moments in the military, but there was even more action in our future. To this day, I cannot believe that the following bizarre event happened next.

We returned to Peachtree Dekalb airport to refuel for our return flight back to Fort Benning. As the aircraft was being serviced, we all decided to grab lunch at the restaurant near the flight line.

After ordering, we all went out on the patio to get some fresh air, when we noticed a nondescript white van traveling at very high speeds directly down the runway toward our position. In a surreal moment, the van crashed into another fuel truck and a parked C-141 Air Force plane.

When the van went airborne during the crash sequence, Hernandez and Prescott, the combat medic and nurse, immediately jumped the fence and took off running towards the crash site. I witnessed that these two didn't even hesitate or recoil. They just ran toward the impact area.

After recognizing what happened, and hesitating, the rest of us took off and followed Prescott and Hernandez. When I arrived at the van, Hernandez and Prescott had already climbed in, without any regard for their personal safety. They entered from the back of the vehicle, even though the strong fumes were alarming, and other fluids like oil, paint and gasoline had been poured throughout the cargo section in an apparent suicide gesture.

The professionalism and bravery of our medical personnel in the military is awesome, and when they take the oath to save lives, it is not cheap talk. I could see from the outside that the driver was slumped forward over the wheel, with his face and upper torso covered in blood. I didn't know if he was dead or alive.

Our two medical folks were working hard to extract the victim from his seatbelt, but it was taking longer than expected. We were very concerned with the fumes, so we started breaking out all of the windows. The two inside thought that the vehicle might explode, so SGT Graves climbed in and helped them extract the victim, and then we all moved away from the impact area and laid him on a tarp. Shortly after they stabilized the victim, all airfield emergency service arrived in force, and took over care of the victim.

The actions of SSG James R. Hernandez and Captain Daniel J. Prescott, and their willingness to lay down their lives for another human exemplifies the very best of humanity...heroism. Their dedication to the cause of saving lives and providing medical care motivated them to operate without regard for their personal risk.

The entire team was later recognized for our actions on that day, and presented awards from a Major General.

Whether it is a local charity, family obligation, faith-based initiative, mentorship, coaching or service to the nation in any capacity, dedication to a cause enriches the human spirit, provides a balanced perspective, and solidifies our purpose in this life.

It was an honor to serve the nation with these amazing soldiers, and all of my fellow soldiers in the U.S. Army. For six years, I was lucky to be a member of the most capable organization on the planet, the U.S. Military.

NEW CHAPTER

Earlier in the book, I discussed some of my experiences in 1994 as part of the Eagle Flight Detachment based on the lovely Mediterranean Island of Cyprus. In addition to adventure and challenge, Cyprus also was the "crack in the door" to exit the Army.

Ironically, the critical moment happened when I least expected it. I was relaxing with three other aircrew members at the beautiful Nissi Beach Resort in Ayia Napa when a friendly gentleman approached us and struck up a conversation.

He told us that he was from Cyprus, but he was studying in New York City at Columbia to earn his MBA, and then he had a job at JP Morgan in Investment Banking.

The four of us, who had flown a mission the previous night into Lebanon, just sat there and listened to this very nice gentleman go on about High Finance, and thought to ourselves, "What the heck is Investment Banking?"

Here we were, four highly trained American aircrew members putting everything on the line every night, to essentially protect the values of freedom, democracy, and capitalism, so dear to Americans, and yet someone who was not from America was telling us all about it. It was an interesting juxtaposition and an idea that I thought about for months.

The majority of my twenty-eight years had been affiliated with the U.S. Army, assuming you take into account my childhood on army installations. I loved the culture, people and camaraderie, but also believed that I should get a slice of the American Pie that this gentleman in Cyprus was snacking on.

I also recognized that my father, who invested 36+ years in dedicated service to the nation, had never become financially savvy, and had not accumulated any meaningful assets.

I returned to my headquarters unit in Germany and began to educate myself on the matriculation process into a top Business School. I left Germany in 1995 and was stationed at Fort Benning (Georgia) in the 498th Medical Evacuation Unit.

The MEDEVAC work schedule, similar to a firefighter's shift, allowed me to utilize the long periods of boredom to prepare for the Graduate Management Admissions Test "GMAT". Additionally, I made the four-hour roundtrip to Atlanta on the weekends to attend the Kaplan Prep course, where I stayed with my sister Bianca.

In the fall of 1995, I was accepted into three top business schools and immediately submitted my paperwork to exit the service.

It was difficult to leave the military community, as it represents the core values that I deeply believe. However, I was also excited about the challenges and opportunities embedded in the future.

In January 1996, at the completion of my contract, I got in my white Ford Ranger truck, and drove away from Fort Benning, Georgia. I had accomplished my dream and served as a UH-60 Blackhawk helicopter pilot for six adventurous years.

I closed the chapter, and headed toward the University of North Carolina at Chapel Hill to open up a new chapter in my life.

Photos

Knee Injury, 1986

College Football, 1987

Ray Ellis Award, 1987

Kent Walker & John Nailor, 1990

John Ramiccio, 1990

Kent Walker, 1990

Matt Weller, 1990

Solo Flight, May 1990

Frank Van Buren

Solo Cycle Chris Jackson, 1990

Instructor Dennis Thorp (RIP) 1990

Graduation, Fort Rucker 1991

Fixing the Hootch, Honduras 1991

Frank Van Buren

Delivering Medical Care, Honduras 1991

Landing Zone (LZ), Honduras 1991

Mountain LZ, Honduras 1991

Tiger Island LZ, Honduras 1991

Frank Van Buren

Girl In Yellow Blouse, Honduras 1991

Community Support, Honduras 1991

White Flag Marking LZ Honduras 1991

Jeff Jepson, Paul Schlett, Bob Hammond, Honduras 1991

Relaxing at Soto Cano AB Honduras. 1991

Mountain LZ Honduras

Fulda Gap, Germany 1993

Chief Warrant Officer James H (Jim) Garst

Stetson Troop, Germany 1992

Air Cavalry, Germany 1992

Water Survival Training, NAS Jax, 1994

Beirut Air Bridge, Mediterranean Sea, 1994

Eagle Flight Detachment, Cyprus 1994

Family, Wingate NC

Faulks Farm, Wingate NC

About the Author

Frank departed the U.S. Army in 1996, and enrolled in the Kenan-Flagler Business School at The University of North Carolina at Chapel Hill where he earned an MBA in 1998.

Frank has worked in the finance industry for over 20 years in Investment Banking and Sales & Trading.

Frank is a professional speaker and life coach www. frankvanburen.com, and lives on a farm in Wingate, North Carolina with his wife Donna and three children.

52922328R00083